The Arts and Social Justice
Re-crafting adult education and community cultural leadership

Dedication

This book is dedicated to the
adult educators who have
given their lives in the
struggle for social justice.

The Arts and Social Justice
Re-crafting adult education and community cultural leadership

Edited by
DARLENE E. CLOVER
AND
JOYCE STALKER

niace
promoting adult learning

© 2007 National Institute of Adult Continuing Education
(England and Wales)

21 De Montfort Street
Leicester
LE1 7GE

Company registration no. 2603322
Charity registration no. 1002775

NIACE has a broad remit to promote lifelong learning opportunities for adults.
NIACE works to develop increased participation in education and training,
particularly for those who do not have easy access because of class, gender,
age, race, language and culture, learning difficulties or disabilities,
or insufficient financial resources.

You can find NIACE online at www.niace.org.uk

Cataloguing in Publication Data
A CIP record of this title is available from the British Library

Designed and typeset by Avon DataSet Ltd, Bidford-on-Avon, Warwickshire
Printed and bound in the UK by Ashford Colour Press, Gosport

ISBN: 978 1 86201 250 9

Contents

Section Four – Art and community development

Contributors

Francesca Albergato-Muterspaw is a Doctoral Candidate in adult education at Pennsylvania State University, Harrisburg, United States. She has a background in musicology and vocal performance and is studying music's role in grieving and the resolution of grief. Francesca has worked in hospices for seven years.

Darlene E. Clover is an Associate Professor in the Faculty of Education, University of Victoria, British Columbia, Canada and a photographer. Her research, teaching and publishing focus on feminist and environmental adult education, community and cultural leadership and the arts. Darlene currently works with street-involved women using murals, poetry, quilting, sculpture, collage and mosaic to explore issues of poverty, health and violence.

Catherine Etmanski is a Doctoral Candidate in the Faculty of Education, University of Victoria, Canada. She is using popular theatre for her PhD research with international and immigrant students to explore issues of racism and connection. Catherine teaches an online course titled *International perspectives in participatory research and evaluation*. She uses film, photography, music and other arts-based media in her work as a community educator, and has organised a number of public exhibitions related to issues of social justice.

Tara Fenwick is a Professor of Education and the new Head of the Educational Studies Department at the University of British Columbia, Canada. But she began her working life as a professional musician. Her primary research and teaching focus on learning, education and identities in work. Her most recent books include *Learning through Experience* (2003), *Work, Subjectivity and Learning* (2006) (co-editors S. Billett and M. Somerville), and *Educating the Global Workforce* (2007) (co-editor Lesley Farrell).

Dr Isabelle Fremeaux is Lecturer in Media Studies at the Faculty of Continuing Education, Birkbeck College, University of London, United Kingdom and a co-founder of the Laboratory of Insurrectionary Imagination (Lab of ii), which aims to help activists and artists to meet, learn from each other and work together. It is as part of the Lab that she has become involved with rebel clowning. Her current research interest focuses on the links between creative forms of activism and popular education in the anti-capitalist 'movement of movements'.

André P. Grace is a Professor engaged in educational policy studies and inclusive education at the University of Alberta. He is currently conducting a national study of the impact of diverse educational interest groups on the accommodation of sexual-minority teachers and students in Canadian schools funded by the Social Sciences and Humanities Research Council of Canada (SSHRC). André and Kristopher Wells are co-authors of an article entitled 'Using Freirean Pedagogy of Just Ire to Inform Critical Social Learning in Arts-Informed Community Education for Sexual Minorities' in *Adult Education Quarterly*, Vol. 57 No. 2.

Anne Kinsella is an assistant professor in the Faculty of Health Sciences at the University of Western Ontario, Canada. Her research interests are health professional education, reflective practice, ethics and aesthetics. Anne studies the ways in which reflection is enacted in professional life to discern action, to foster personal and professional knowledge development, to inform ethical practice, and to promote social justice. The author gratefully acknowledges support for this work from the Social Sciences and Humanities Research Council of Canada.

Penne Lane is a doctoral candidate in Adult Education at the University of Georgia, USA. Her research centres on handicraft production in mountain cultures around the world, particularly Appalachian and East European mountain regions. She is interested in the intersections of adult education and international development and in challenging the expansion of neo-liberal economics and the social inequalities it produces.

Hilary Ramsden is a performer, adult educator, co-artistic director of Walk and Squawk Performance Project, and member of the Laboratory of Insurrectionary Imagination (Lab of ii). She sees her work as a particular (and possibly peculiar) blend of live and relational art, clown, movement and 'artivism' that is a result and expression of her belief in the power of art to transform our lives. She is currently involved in practice-based research exploring rupture and dislocation through walking and rebel clowning and is a Masters student at Goldsmiths College, University of London, United Kingdom.

Joyce Stalker is Associate Professor/Reader at the University of Waikato, Aotearoa New Zealand. Her current research area weaves together her first degree in textiles science and design, her feminist beliefs and her view that the key role of adult education is to foster social justice. The stories in the three publications which she and Darlene co-edited are encouraging Joyce to move her sewing into the realm of fabric protest.

Kristopher Wells is a Canada Graduate Scholar and a Killam Doctoral Scholar who researches sexual-minority inclusion in educational policy and practice. He recently developed the Alberta Teachers' Association's *Sexual Orientation and Gender Identity* educational website, which can be accessed at http://www.teachers.ab.ca. His area of specialisation is the effects of arts-informed, community-based informal education on youth development, socialisation, and resiliency.

Nora West trained in creative embroidery and fabric-print at Goldsmiths College, London. She has had numerous solo shows, and worked as a tertiary lecturer, curator, arts writer and convener of the New Zealand Creative Spaces Network. Nora also co-ran a community banner-making practice, Flying Colours, which included making protest banners for peace and environmental causes. Currently she teaches art in prisons, and advises on arts access projects for the Auckland Main Street programme.

Foreword

I'm not sure how many adult educators will read this book. A further consequence of the neo-liberal, corporate insanity that has turned a generation of teachers and learners alike into target-meeters, form-fillers and box-tickers, has been the reduction of challenging ideas, complex arguments and imaginative re-constructions of what is usually taken for granted into bullet points and bite-sized chunks: to be quickly digested and easily forgotten. It seems there are just too many books, and too little time.

But everyone who cares about adult education as a force for progressive social change, and a resource for what Raymond Williams called 'a journey of hope', should take some time to read and think about what follows here. Not least because, in their collective enthusiasm for aesthetic ways of knowing and for the power of the Arts to stimulate radical learning and strengthen cultural democracy, the authors provide a welcome escape from the dreary, instrumental, and increasingly coercive, preoccupation with skills for work and crowd control that so much routine practice in 'Western' countries has now become.

These are accounts of learning through singing, weaving, perform-ance, quilt-making, embroidery, literature, poetry, banner-making, and rebel-clowning. Their main purpose is not to teach an artistic skill for individual gain, or for recreational purposes, although both of these aspects may well provide pleasure and give satisfaction to those involved. But rather, in the activity of creativity, to address complex contemporary issues such as violence against women, gender discrimination, cultural imperialism, racism, poverty and other economic imbalances; as well as becoming producers and communicators, as distinct from passive consumers, of culture. What follows gives wonderful insights into how different educators have found exciting and subversive ways of turning art into a politicising act, that helps adults make sense of their concerns, create meaning in their lives and contribute to the re-creation of a better world.

You don't need to be an arts educator to draw inspiration from this book. Its message – about the need to recognise disobedience, alternative knowledge, creativity, pleasure, metaphor and action, in the pursuit of social justice and social transformation – is a timely lesson for what currently counts as adult education in a troubled and divided world.

Jane Thompson

Introduction

Darlene E. Clover and Joyce Stalker

A defiant imagination . . . defies the constraints of expectation and the everyday . . . because the imagination – liberated by engagement with cultural expression – is necessary to the achievement of all we hope for as a society.

Canadian Literary Artist, Max Wyman

Neo-liberal political, economic, social and educational policies create major challenges for adult educators committed to the social and political purpose of learning. As these agendas create acute problems of justice, equity and critical learning, one positive force to which we can turn is the critical imagination. *The arts and social justice: Re-crafting adult education and community cultural leadership* is an attempt to map some of the innovative and critical arts-based pedagogies which adult educators are using in formal and non-formal settings. They are used to facilitate the creative learning and leadership required to meet the complex, multi-layered political, economic, social, cultural and educational challenges in our contemporary neo-liberal worlds. Working with and through the aesthetic dimension, educators have found an exciting and alternative way to help adults make sense of their worlds, create meaning in their lives and re-create a better world.

The arts and social justice: Re-crafting adult education and community cultural leadership is grounded in the understanding that the arts matter in our lives, in adult education and learning and in bringing about social justice and transformation. Using arts, crafts and other symbolic, performative, metaphoric and visual forms the adult educators featured

I

in this volume address complex contemporary issues such as violence against women and gender discrimination, homophobia, racism, poverty and other economic imbalances, fear and suspicion instilled in communities around what Fremeaux and Ramsden in this volume refer to as 'ill-defined terrorists', declines in active civic engagement and involvement, questions of identity and challenges to health and the ethic of care.

These stories demonstrate how and why engaging the aesthetic dimension enhances, or has the potential to enhance, transformative, democratic and emancipatory objectives of adult education. The authors challenge the idea of adult education as simply rational discursive modes which interpret experience. Rather, they draw attention to the imagination as a power of cognition and medium for alternative meaning-making and expression. Linking theory, practice, research or policy work in critical, creative and practical ways, this collection provides an aesthetic, cultural lens through which we can view learning, teaching, advocacy and activism.

Arts-based adult education, as articulated in this book, is an imagin-ative, participatory and critical approach to personal, political, economic, social and cultural transformation. It is based on working and learning collectively through artistic processes to develop new paradigms for comprehending and valuing culture and people's aesthetic selves, promoting consciousness and knowledge, stimulating imaginative critique, re-constructing and re-positioning cultural identity, strengthening cultural democracy and community leadership, enhancing people's abilities to challenge processes and practices that exclude, marginalise and disempower and new paradigms which foster social action. As Albergato-Muterspaw and Fenwick suggest in this volume, arts-based adult education and learning provokes radical and creative visions of an alternative world – as if things could be otherwise – a hopeful goal much required in these neo-liberal times.

Inspiration behind this book

The arts and adult education are old and familiar partners.
Canadian adult educator, J. Roby Kidd

This book was inspired by a study we undertook over a three-year period that amplified for us the power, potential and challenge of the creative yet critical educational medium called the arts. The research seemed to be telling us that although the arts in adult education were by no means new, as J. Roby Kidd points out in the above quotation, they were in fact, growing and diversifying. When in 2005 we sent out a call for articles for a special edition of the international adult education journal, *Convergence*, our suspicions (dare we say 'hopes'?) were confirmed. The response was overwhelming, representing this contemporary groundswell of creative and aesthetic practices; the submissions too many for a single journal but the voices too valuable to be lost to the field of adult education. As a result, we have now published a trilogy: a special issue (Social justice, arts and adult education) of *Convergence* Vol. 38 No. 4 in 2005; a special edition of the *New Zealand Journal of Adult Learning* Vol. 34 No. 4 in 2006; and this edited volume. Articles chosen for *Convergence* aimed at practitioners around the globe. Those for the *New Zealand Journal of Adult Learning* shared research findings and methodologies. For this book, we identified works that would have universal appeal to theoreticians, researchers and practitioners.

Aim of the book and a note on the authors

Art is on the side of the oppressed. Think before you shudder at the simplistic dictum and its heretical definition of the freedom of art. For if art is freedom of the spirit, how can it exist within the oppressors?
American Literary Artist, Edith Wharton

The overall aim of this book is to highlight arts-based adult education theorising, research and practice in various parts of the world that honour the aesthetic dimension of the human being and make the links between the arts, education and social justice by using culture as a tool and site of critical, social learning. An objective is to show how arts-based adult education and learning opportunities enlarge people's creative capacities, enhance cultural community leadership and encourage new aesthetic forms of civic engagement. Drawing upon an array of visual, graphic, textile, textual, aural, embodied and poetic practices, the chapters highlight the role the medium of arts plays in mitigating some of the dehumanising effects of neo-liberalism and globalisation. They thus make a creative and critical contribution to the contemporary practice and theory of adult education. It is our hope that by reading this book, practitioners, researchers, scholars, educator-activists and community-based artists will better understand the potential of the arts (and we include crafts as an art). We hope we all will better understand them as a way to reclaim knowledge and tradition, promote democracy and identity, raise consciousness, promote gender equity, stimulate imaginative power, challenge oppression and injustices and encourage women and men to take control of the decisions that affect their lives.

The contributors to this book are scholars/professors, researchers, community educators, students, community-based artists and activists. In many cases we wear more than one hat. The arts-based practices we highlight include quilting and other fabric arts, crafts, storytelling, literature, poetry, music, drama/theatre, graffiti, and clowning. They/we are located in communities or universities in Canada, New Zealand, the United Kingdom and the United States. The majority of the authors are women and many put forward an aesthetic feminist perspective we hope readers will find re-invigorating in today's neo-liberal climate of back-lash. While confining this book to experiences from Western countries may miss an opportunity to highlight the valuable practices, voices, and insights of those who make up the majority world, the issues, tensions, art practices, theories and challenges will have universal resonance.

Structure of the book

> Be aware of the courage and persistence that it has taken for these
> images and these words to be shared so bravely.
>
> Canadian arts-based researcher, Helen Ball

This book is divided into four sections that reflect conceptual understandings and themes that underpin the arts and/in adult education.
There are two chapters within each section and each is a tapestry of
noise, energy, image, symbol, metaphor, ideas and action. The book as a
whole weaves these together into a creative message of strategy, learning,
educative-activism and engagement.

Teaching and learning art

> Our strategy should be not only to confront the empire but to mock
> it . . . with our art . . . our stubbornness, our joy, our brilliance, our
> sheer relentlessness.
>
> Indian literary artist-activist, Arundhati Roy

Teaching and learning are fundamental to adult education. Within the
realm of the arts, teaching and learning are most often associated with
learning an artistic skill – to sculpt, act, or play the piano. Problematically,
however, the arts, and particularly women's arts, are often seen simply as
"a charming end product" (Stalker, 2003, p. 27). Worse yet, the arts and
adult education are also associated with what Yeomans (1995) refers to
as "recreational evening classes where elderly ladies and gentlemen paint
pretty pictures of flowers and landscapes from their favourite postcards"
(p. 219). The result of this was the banishment of arts and imagination in
education to a category of frivolity, an ontological homelessness of scorn
and condescension (Shakotko & Walker, 1999).

Isabelle Fremeaux and Hilary Ramsden, rebels with an aesthetic-
political cause, provide a dynamic re-framing of teaching and learning
arts. They focus on the ancient practice of rebel clowning, a form of arts
and political activism they call 'artivism'. As an exploration of authoritarianism through parody and ridicule, learning the art of rebel clowning
stimulates creative, embodied ways of addressing complex issues such as
coercion, self-censorship and inhibition whilst releasing the subversive

power of play and humour. Rebel clowning, a carnival form of joyful resistance, encourages a discovery of peoples' capacities for creatively stimulating radical social change. The authors provide in-depth descriptions of training workshops in clowning, buffoonery and storytelling as well as techniques such as 'name switch' and 'hug tag' that disrupt processes of logical thinking.

Anne Kinsella, in the second chapter in this section, provides an insightful look into how learning literature makes connections between concrete things, such as illness, and abstract things, such as healthcare. In the face of the growing medicalisation and de-personalisation of health care in Canada, Kinsella's argument is that literary arts make an important contribution to educating socially-responsive, aware and caring practitioners. Through her own experiences of reading and re-reading texts she explores the potential which stories and literature have to foster new ways of seeing, feeling and understanding, to promote praxis and, most importantly, to assist health educators and professionals to re-engage with and to reconstruct their lifeworlds.

The emancipatory potential of arts-based adult education

> The desire to make image and communicate something of the otherwise unsayable is innate in all of us.
>
> British art educator, Colin Rhodes

Concepts of emancipation and empowerment are fundamental to feminist, adult education and arts-based discourses. Walters and Manicom (1996) worry, however, that given their 'extensive use and appropriation by a very broad range of political positions [they have] been drained of any clear referent and, in many contexts, of [their] more politically transformative meaning' (p. 16).

André Grace and Kristopher Wells bring us back into that more politically transformative meaning in their chapter. They describe and analyse their arts-informed educational work with lesbian, gay, bisexual, trans-identified, two-spirited, queer, and allied (LGBTTQ&A) youth and young adults. Camp fYrefly in Edmonton, Alberta is a mentoring programme which, through a variety of practices such as popular theatre, poetry, autobiography and graffiti, builds the artistic and social agency and identity of the youth by encouraging their leadership skills and creative ways of knowing. Weaving poetry and narrative vignettes throughout the text, Grace and Wells explore queer bodies and queer theory in terms of positionalities within the camp and the larger cultural milieu of the young people. Their multi-perspective theorising juxtaposes critical ethnography and post-modern aesthetics with arts-based inquiry and provides an aesthetic through which we can view anti-oppression work.

Darlene Clover's chapter re-situates quilting as a critical social practice of feminist adult education. She tells the story of a four-phase quilting project on sexual exploitation that originated on Vancouver Island, British Columbia, moved to an international conference in Vancouver and then came back to Vancouver Island for completion. Through the lens of feminist aesthetic theory and adult education, Clover explores the ways in which this quilting process encouraged risk-taking around the volatile issue of sexual exploitation and how the aesthetic oppositional messages and counter-messages woven into the imagery of the quilt destabilise fixed ideas and uncover complexities. Key elements of this type of artistic practice are its mobility, its ability to foster both individual and social empowerment, and the layer it adds to the process-versus-product debate in feminist adult education.

Arts-based adult learning and democracy

> Through their creative work [people] have changed the world and the history of forms of human, imaginative expression is the history of human civilisation itself.
>
> British adult educator, Bill Williamson

The history of democracy is a struggle to assert rights and to seek balance, inclusion, justice and equity as citizens. Developing educational practices that challenge women and men to promote, and more fully participate in, the democratic process is central to adult education. Many adult educators believe that unless education is linked to larger struggles and strategies it will lose many of its aspirations to social justice and transformation. Welton (1995) adds that we must resort to advocacy, activism and politics because 'not all issues are amenable to resolution through rational discourse' (p. 68).

Catherine Etmanski's chapter is an insightful analysis of a creative practice of democracy – Legislative Theatre (LT) – as taught in Vancouver, Canada by the non-profit theatre company Headlines Theatre. LT is a process by which decision-making bodies use forum theatre as a means of public consultation. In the case presented by Etmanski, LT is used to pose questions around diminishing social services, and provide the Vancouver City Council with a creative report that contained no less than 90 policy recommendations. The chapter discusses some of the challenges that emerged during the policy implementation phase, and resulting philosophical and practical considerations for LT practitioners such as ensuring an appropriate process for policy implementation is in place at the outset to solidify LT as a legitimate form of practising democracy.

A key point Nora West and Joyce Stalker make in their chapter is that cultural democracy is as important as political and social democracy. And cultural democracy only flourishes in societies where wide participation in the arts is encouraged and artworks are valued not solely for their aesthetic nature but also for their therapeutic and social functions. This chapter explores twenty-five years of connections amongst social movements, artist–educators, the fabric craft world, and the development of Aotearoa New Zealand identity against a backdrop of colonisation. Using examples of fabric craft practices and the stories of indigenous and non-indigenous artists, West and Stalker highlight artists and their fabric crafts as instigators and perpetuators of cultural democracy and leadership.

Art and community development

> Aesthetic forms are important because they signify and encapsulate a society's structure of feeling and this tacit, underlying way of seeing and responding to one's circumstances contributes to forms of consciousness.
>
> American art educator, Landon Beyer

Chapters in the fourth section of this book fall under a category of long-established practice in the field of both adult education and arts and adult education – community development. On the one hand, we can understand community development within its economic context. This framing constitutes an important aspect of adult education as 'global economic forces have increased the number of people living in poverty and undermined traditional ways of life and livelihoods' (Jongeward, 1994 p. 83). On the other hand, we can also understand community development as an 'alternative route' (Van der Veen 2003, p. 581) to education and learning that builds unity in community, however community is defined. In brief, community development is, ideally, a process in which people identify and use their resources and strengths to create healthy, economically-strong communities.

For musicians and adult educators Francesca Albergato-Muterspaw and Tara Fenwick, music and singing are creative alternative routes to community development. They emphasise the importance of music in cultural animation and show how song has for centuries been woven with adult learning. Music has served as a medium for transmitting information, sharing stories and binding communities by enculturating norms and values or generating resistance. Although often given less attention as one of the arts in adult education, music, song and community choirs have for centuries provided a forum through which people within social movements and communities come together and experience communion in powerful emotional and aesthetic ways. As a way of knowing, music acts as a harmonious communicative practice which requires no special equipment, talent, or able-ness.

Penne Lane focuses in her chapter on the concept of economic justice vis-à-vis art production and commodification. How does a community balance crafts as a cultural emblem with its role as a source of livelihood? What learning is required to confront economic efforts that force artisans into mass craft production? Using the metaphor of a four-harness loom, Lane explores the intersections of historical context, life experiences, neo-liberalism, and other contemporary social and cultural transformations in the lives of women artisans in the Appalachian region of the United States and the Carpathian mountain region of western Ukraine. Using Tanya's story, Lane describes how women in the Ukraine resist the commodification of their handicrafts by joining together to learn alternative ways to make a living for themselves and their families. Linda's story from the Appalachia region highlights a cultural leader determined to educate people around the value of crafts and work to create a strong, 'just' infrastructure for selling their work. Lane argues that by making connections to artisans, as Miles Horton of the Highlander Centre did, adult educators can assist them with challenges they face.

Threads and tensions

> The subversive stitch can be viewed as a motif that disrupts, or as a motivation to disrupt. But is the narrative really disrupted by the sewing? Or does the sewing make the story visible?
>
> Canadian Fabric Artist, Mireille Perron

We conclude this chapter with a discussion of six further threads and tensions woven throughout the fabric of this book. They build on the above themes but raise and represent additional critical questions within the contemporary field of arts-based adult education for social justice. These threads and tensions often intersect, overlap or relate to each other in ways which suggest different concepts and terms are being used to address complex yet somewhat similar issues in a globalised, neo-liberal world. Many respond to complex questions within the field of the arts as well as adult education but there is always a unique aesthetic and cultural dimension to the theorising. Our intention in the section that follows is to stimulate reflection and debate in the hope that readers will take-up the threads and weave their own fabrics of arts-based adult education.

Individual versus social/collective learning

Tension has long existed between the individual or personal, and the social or collective learning purposes of adult education, particularly given the vocational and apolitical thrust that undermines the field (Thompson, 2002). The same is true within the scope of the arts and arts-based adult educators Elias, Jones and Normie (1995) shape the debate like this:

> the purposes of adult education in the arts . . . can be categorised in terms of two broad areas of activity concerned with either the individual or with society; they are either concerned with the development of the individual or they are concerned to maintain or reinforce a dominant culture or to change and develop it. (p. 9)

There is a strong tendency towards individual creativity and expression over collective, social efforts to use the arts as a tool for change. The question often arises as to whether or not it is actually art if it is not solely a free form of individual creative self-expression. Yet it is possible to operate from both perspectives in both the arts and adult education. Feminist adult educators believe that fostering both the person and the social is imperative (Walters & Manicom, 1996) whilst feminist art theorists work to legitimise collective practices of political or activist art as 'art' (e.g. Felshin, 1995).

Within this book, there is a tension between self-growth as an important process that is not necessarily an end in itself, and social justice and change as a fundamental goal of adult learning that cannot be reached without creating healthy and empowered individuals. For example, many stories pay attention to and encourage individual growth particularly in cases where women and LGBTTQ&A youth and young adults have suffered some form of social violence or exploitation (Clover; Grace & Wells) or where an anti-globalisation protester begins to feel a deep sense of powerlessness (Fremeaux & Ramsden). Yet these and other chapters also actively address the issue of belonging to, and participating in, the larger social world. Community choirs function as spaces where individuals come together for change. Crafters are individualised in Lane's chapter but there is an underlying ethos of a collective economic injustice that can only be cured by working and learning together. Clowns are professionals in their own right but collectively, they are a powerful social force. The contemporary professionalisation of the health industry that all but eliminates an ethic of care demands a new form of education and learning that re-links practitioners to the lifeworld. It is this inter-weaving of the individual/personal and the social/collective that makes such a powerful and positive platform of arts-based adult education. Clover presents a slightly different framing of personal/collective through the quilt. It is made up of individual squares that represent personal stories and voices, but the discussions that took place while creating the squares, and putting it together as one tapestry, become a collective story and identity. In all the chapters, there is an indefatigable belief that collective aesthetics are valid as arts.

Product and process

Closely related to the above, and probably as constant, is the process-versus-product debate in adult education and the arts field. There are two premises behind this debate. The first comes from the neo-liberal framework of consumption and consumerism. It situates art as a product or good to be valued for its ability to be possessed or its commercial value, rather than for its socio-cultural meaningfulness and political utility (Lury, 1999).

The second premise behind the process-product debate is embedded within education. Whereas learning is seen as fluid and evolving, the product is often viewed as static and of lesser importance. This debate, although at times more nuanced and taking an artistic turn, is an important theme in this book, tackling both perspectives and demonstrating the tensions. We see this tension in Grace and Wells' chapter. They state that process is more valuable than the art product in terms of empowering LGBTTQ&A and yet they draw attention to the importance of making the artwork public in order to enable communion among the youth and various audiences. We also see the tensions in the chapter by Fremeaux and Ramsden who adamantly stress the importance of training in the preparation of 'clownbattents' and yet seem to place equal value on the skill and ability – the product of the training – required to connect more fully with the audience and make the tactic actually work. Albergato-Muterspaw and Fenwick stress that no ability to sing is required to be part of a choir and that the most important element is the togetherness. But underlying this is the fact that community choirs are not cacophonies but rather melodious harmonising which captivates the audience.

In the three cases above, the authors are talking about 'the public', 'the audience' and it is this factor which helps us to understand the tension between process and product. The work of Headlines Theatre shows that engaging in popular theatre at the political level means realising that the product and process must have equal value as much of the power of this work comes from it being very good theatre. Good theatre means professionally-done theatre, although it does begin with so-called amateurs who become artist-actors for change. This emphasis on professionalism prevents the work from being diminished on artistic merit (even if some are not happy with the social framing). The artisans in Lane's chapter struggle for quality over quantity as this is the key to their collective identity as craftswomen. But they also aim to sell their goods as commodities and this complements the economic-justice framework which Lane applies. Kinsella argues that the outcome or product of learning through literature must be more sensitive, caring and empathetic health care practitioners if we are to mitigate the dehumanising effects of professional health care. Clover, like Headlines Theatre, shows how the quality of the quilts must be recognised and validated by the viewer in order to strengthen its ability to convey a difficult message. If an artwork is created for solely personal, therapeutic reasons, the issue of quality may not be as relevant. But when a work is made public, when it becomes a tool of social learning and justice, its quality often seems to be key to its impact as well as the esteem of the artist/creator.

Aesthetic agency and cultural identity

Identity and agency are critical to adult education theory and practice. One of the characteristics that differentiate the authors in this collection is how they approach these issues in terms of the aesthetic and cultural dimension they add to the discourse. Lane shows how cultural agency – taking control of the production of handicrafts – strengthens women as actors and artists in Ukrainian and American societies. It is the act of learning together to be artists and choosing how and where their arts will be made and sold that creates the strongest sense of a collective cultural identity. For Grace and Wells, a 'queer' cultural identity and agency means a fluid identity which positions LGBTTQ&A youth as narrators of and actors in their own stories. West and Stalker show the value and place of fabric crafts in the development of an Aotearoa New Zealand identity as it emerges from and within British and bicultural heritages as well as new multi-cultural dimensions. An important idea behind the quilting project in Clover's chapter is to move beyond an identity of 'victim of exploitation' towards being creative artists and actors with the ability to not only name but re-imagine themselves within the larger social struggle opposing violence against women.

Another way in which the authors present agency and identity in this collection is through the lens of being and becoming artists. The youth and young adults in the chapter by Grace and Wells blossom as they become poets while the rebel clowns feel their power when the audience laughs and identifies with their personas. Albergato-Muterspaw and Fenwick highlight how music deliberately sets out to mix people of different cultural and social backgrounds together building a stronger collective, cultural identity. West and Stalker perhaps state it best when they note that when people bring creative works of art into existence they become active producers and transmitters of culture and identity, rather than simply passive consumers of a ready-made, often culturally homogeneous world.

Community cultural leadership

Linked to the above is the stronger connection being made in adult education between learning, agency, actors of and for change and the concept of leadership (Clover, 2007; Fenwick, Nesbit & Spencer, 2006; Walters & Manicom, 1996). A common thread or theme in the chapters, although approached from different angles, is the idea of community cultural leadership. The first angle is the artist as educator-leader. We see particularly in the writings of West and Stalker an emphasis on the role of artists as leaders in terms of creating and defining a nation and teaching people who they are, and who they might become. Albergato-Muterspaw and Fenwick re-position musicians as leaders within social movements and choirs as their tools to build community. Etmanski's tale of Headlines Theatre is a case study of cultural leadership. People use the arts to negotiate a complex network of power relations in order to work together to create policy and bring about change in legislative processes. The basic premise is that we must resort to creativity, not solely rational discourse, to strengthen participatory democracy. It is about artists who re-craft report writing and policy recommendations. Kinsella demonstrates a type of cultural leadership in terms of re-shaping the ways in which health professionals are educated. This leadership directly challenges traditional forms of health education which disregard the arts as a positive medium for learning.

The second aspect of cultural leadership is training cultural leaders. Grace and Wells' work aims to develop what they refer to as transformative leaders, youths who can inspire others to come forward and let their voices be heard. Cultural leadership can therefore be defined as using an arts medium to develop an aesthetic, cultural voice, sense of identity and consciousness and actor or agent of change in community or society. It is not, as Fremeaux and Ramsden stress, a process of leadership where expertise is transferred but rather a process of working together, artist, educator and community, as co-agents for democratic, social and cultural change.

The defiant imagination

Current practices of neo-liberalism aim towards a unified world – a single or universal mode of production, political framework, language, culture and practice of education – in order to bring about the organic integration of a single economy and logic. Neo-liberalism reduces the provision of services and vocationalises education in order to 'encourage citizens to become more self-sufficient consumers or customers' (Martin, 2003, p. 568). Flow-on consequences of this include an acceptance of individualism, competitiveness, and inequalities coupled with a frightening homogenisation or uniformity.

A defiant imagination for Wyman (2004) has the ability to defy these constraints and therefore becomes a major hope for the diversification and re-orientation of society. A defiant imagination allows for the conception and creation of counter-narratives of protest and resistance and opportunities for alternative analysis and reflection (Clover & Markle, 2003). Throughout the book we see instances of the imagination breaking out to challenge racism, inequality and injustice. Kinsella introduces us to the concept of 'moral imagination'. By this she does not mean moralising at the expense of rights or as justification for brutality and domination, practices that seem to be dominating the world stage. Rather, her linking of morality and imagination springs from literature that enables new forms of decision-making, involves choice, and becoming more compassionate and sensitised to ethical uses of power and disability or illness experiences. The quilt in Clover's chapter is a defiant discursive tapestry of oppositional and counter messages that creatively, through design, colour, and image, destabilise fixed ideas and highlight dichotomies and structural inequities. The imaginative antics of the clowns in Fremeaux and Ramsden's chapter defy the official restrictions placed upon protesters. West and Stalker show how the defiant imagination of a nation is throwing off the shackles of colonisation and developing a new cultural identity.

Limitations

In diverse ways all the authors address the limitations of arts-based adult education. Etmanski draws attention to the limitations of legislative theatre in terms of its impact on policy. No matter how creatively crafted, participatory or defiant, measures to change structures of power do not necessarily work. Grace and Wells warn that although arts-based inquiry and learning can contribute to self-esteem and knowledge building, unless they are informed by an ethic of care, they could be quite damaging to people who have been marginalised by society. Mixing art 'therapy' and education can sometimes lead to situations which hurt rather than help. Lane is quick to point out that craft work undertaken outside the mainstream commodified market can be a licence for poverty and exclusion while West and Stalker lament the delegitimisation of fabric crafts in the face of male-dominated sports. When using literature, there is always the danger of the 'fact' and 'fiction' dichotomy. Kinsella reminds us that we need to take care in terms of the quality and the relationship between the subjectivity of the individual and the text. She is also quick to point out that although some see the potential of learning through literary texts, this approach in health professional education is still widely viewed as a subversive tactic rather than a valid practice. Clover raises the issue of censorship in the arts as a limitation. It silences and marginalises work that dares to challenge normative beliefs or work outside established conventions. But, as risk and challenge are the essence of adult learning, censorship can also be seen as an important learning moment because it speaks to the power of an artwork to challenge the status quo and make people think, discuss, debate and sometimes, act.

Final words

> As we grow older, we should become not less radical but more so.
> Canadian literary artist, Margaret Lawrence

At the heart of this book is the belief that paying attention to the aesthetic and cultural dimensions of humans and their lifeworlds is paramount to efforts to develop politically-oriented emancipatory and critical pedagogies. These, in turn, can play a key role in countering the harmful effects of neo-liberalism, globalisation and the instrumental-isation and rationalisation of adult learning.

Our hope is that this volume will stimulate reflection and debate, and encourage more adult educators to re-craft their approaches to include creative arts-based pedagogies and the critical, social imagination of adults. As this publication demonstrates, the arts clearly have a strong potential to strengthen the struggle for social justice. Together, we will not leave that potential untapped.

References

Clover, D. E. (2007) 'From sea to cyberspace: Women's leadership and learning around information and communication technologies in coastal Newfoundland', *International Journal of Lifelong Education*, Vol. 26, No. 1, pp. 75–88.

Clover, D. E. and Markle G. (2003) 'Feminist arts practices of popular education: Imagination, counter-narratives and activism on Vancouver Island and Gabriola Island', *New Zealand Journal of Adult Learning*, Vol. 31, No. 2, pp. 36–52.

Elias, W., Jones, D. and Normie, G. (1995) *Truth without facts, selected papers from the first three international conferences on adult education and the arts.* Brussels: VUBPress.

Felshin, N. (ed) (1995) *But is it art? The spirit of art as activism.* Seattle: Bay Press.

Fenwick, T., Nesbit, T. and Spencer, B. (eds) (2006) *Contexts of adult education: Canadian perspectives*, Toronto: Thompson Educational Publishing.

Jongeward, C. (1994) 'Connecting with creative process: Adult learning through art making within a supportive community'. In T. Sork (ed), *Theory and practice, CASAE conference proceedings* (pp. 237–42). Vancouver: Simon Fraser University.

Lury, C. (1999) *Consumer culture.* Oxford: Polity Press.

Martin, I. (2003) 'Adult education, lifelong learning and citizenship: Some ifs and buts', *International Journal of Lifelong Education*, Vol. 22, No. 6, pp. 566–79.

Shakotko, D. and Walker, K. (1999) 'Poetic leadership'. In P. Begley and P. Leonard (eds), *The values of educational administration* (pp. 201–22). London: Falmer Press.

Stalker, J. (1996) 'The new right and adult educators: A feminist view', *Access Critical Perspectives on Cultural and Policy Studies in Education*, Vol. 15, No. 2, pp. 67–79.

Stalker, J. (2003) ' "Ladies' work" and feminist critical pedagogy'. In D. Flowers (ed), *Proceedings of the forty-fourth Adult Education Research Conference* (pp. 399–404). San Francisco: SF State University.

Thompson, J. (2002) *Bread and roses: Arts, culture and lifelong learning*. Leicester: NIACE.

Van der Veen, R. (2003) 'Community development as citizen education', *International Journal of Lifelong Education*, Vol. 22, No. 6, pp. 580–96.

Walters, S. and Manicom, L. (1996) *Gender and adult education*. London: Zed Books.

Welton, M. R. (ed) (1995) *In defense of the lifeworld: Critical perspectives on adult learning*. New York: State University of New York Press.

Wyman, M. (2004) *Why culture matters: The defiant imagination*. Vancouver/Toronto: Douglas & McIntyre.

Yeomans, R. (1995) 'Adult art education as a subversive activity'. In W. Elias, D. Jones and G. Normie (eds), *Truth without facts, selected papers from the first three international conferences on adult education and the arts* (pp. 219–28). Brussels: VUBPress.

Section One

Teaching and learning art

CHAPTER I

We disobey to love

Rebel clowning for social justice

Isabelle Fremeaux and Hilary Ramsden

Introduction

Scotland, July 2005. Anti-G8 mobilisations. A small group of clowns is making its way to the G8 Alternatives march. They pass over a bridge above the motorway. Half a dozen policemen line up, they face the line of clowns and stare at each other. Two clowns start to count down: "three, two, one – go!". The police and clowns rush towards each other, the clowns' hands are outstretched and, faces grimacing, the clowns scream "Kazamm!". There is a floating moment of confusion . . . and they run into each others' open arms. Clowns hug policemen, police-men hug clowns. Everyone is a bit surprised, there is a roar of celebra-tory cheers from the clowns and slightly sheepish and embarrassed applause from the police . . . Somehow, this group of clowns managed to persuade the police to play a game with them. Known as Goblins, Wizards and Giants, it is a version of paper-scissor-stone, but played in teams with the whole body. One of the rules is that if both teams choose the same character, no one wins and they all have to hug. This is exactly what happened as clowns and police simultaneously chose to be 'wizards'. In other words, this is a magic moment of rebel clowning.

The neo-liberal order seems to be on a mission to capture our imagination and transform everything it touches into an object of consumption by playing on our insecurities and fear. The discourse of terror and multi-polar threats is omnipresent: from ill-defined terrorists to so-called anti-social teenagers and invading asylum-seekers, the world is increasingly depicted as a threatening place where the origin of the threat in question is ever-fuzzy, and civil liberties are seized in the name of security.

More generally the neo-liberal order reinforces the structures of oppression that epitomise our society. Patriarchy, racism, homophobia and class oppression consolidate a pervasive authoritarianism that is rooted in and contributes to a paralysis of imagination and a channelling of creativity towards the sustainability of the system itself rather than personal empowerment and liberation. We increasingly live in a society which, as well as exploiting ordinary people, tightly controls creativity and imagination whilst simultaneously repressing dissidence.

Such context has led to the emergence, over the last decade, of the so-called anti-capitalist movement, which has demonstrated a capacity to reinvent political actions and communication. It does this through a creative, symbolic language, often carnivalesque and satirical, away from the traditional communiqués and rallies of the Old Left.

This 'movement of movements' (Klein, 2002) is about imagination, creativity and disobedience and takes the streets as its main frame of action, without lobbying, without negotiating with authorities. It privileges Direct Action to reclaim the commons which have been enclosed and commodified by capitalism and to struggle against the roots of inequalities generated by the system. Drawing on anarchist traditions, Direct Action is literally direct and unmediated. It does not aim to generate publicity or influence policy process but to directly change society. This is clearly expressed in a 1996 leaflet distributed by Reclaim the Streets!, an important Direct Action group in the 1990s, which organised non-authorised street parties to articulate issues around the domination of public spaces by cars and consumerism (and by extension the notion of anti-capitalism). The one-page leaflet states that:

> Direct action actually enables people to develop a new sense of self-confidence and an awareness of their individual and collective power. Direct action is founded on the idea that people can develop the ability for self-rule only through practice, and proposes that all persons directly decide the important issues facing them. Direct action is not just a tactic; it is individuals asserting their ability to control their own lives and to participate in social life without the need for mediation or control by bureaucrats or professional politicians. Direct action

encompasses a whole range of activities, from organizing co[-]ops to engaging in resistance to authority. Direct action places moral commitment above positive law. Direct action is not a last resort when other methods have failed, but the preferred way of doing things.

(Reclaim the streets! 1996)

It is within this framework that the practice of rebel clowning in the United Kingdom is situated. Developed for people to creatively engage in social change, rebel clowning is a form of radical political activism that brings together the ancient art of clowning and the more recent practice of non-violent direct action. It is a practice that transforms and sustains the emotional life of those engaged in social change – seeing both the soul and the street as sites of struggle – as well as being an effective tool for direct action. At the core of this approach is the notion that innovative forms of creative street action are crucial for inspiring and building movements, and simultaneously involve a deeper process that 'liberates people with weapons of love and laughter' (www.clownarmy.org).

An exploration of authoritarianism through parody and ridicule, this practice aims to tap into participants' creativity and imagination to address issues of coercion, self-censorship and inhibition, and release the subversive power of play within each individual. This is developed in specially devised training sessions which use clowning and story-telling, to prepare participants to become 'clownbattants' with the Clandestine Insurgent Rebel Clown Army (also known as CIRCA) or simply to apply the principles in their daily lives and communities.

This chapter is the result of an action research project by five of the core members who devised the practice between early 2004 and the summer of 2005. We engaged in several cycles of action-reflection (plan-act-observe-reflect) and we triangulated our methods of data gathering by combining participant observation, journal entries, interviews and group discussions. Two of us were particularly interested in disseminating some of our findings. We begin this chapter by outlining the key features of rebel clowning: its carnivalesque spirit and the resulting re-appropriation of our 'docile bodies' through trans-gression and unpredictability. Then we reflect on the actual training and examine the various ways in which it offers a framework for collective exploration. We show how this training follows in the tradition of radical adult education and aims to promote embodied learning and critical (self-) understanding so that participants feel empowered to struggle against all forms of oppression.

Key features

As a form that clearly posits the necessity for creative approaches to the way one engages in resisting the neo-liberal order, rebel clowning draws on several major practices and has a variety of inspirations. One of the most important is the notion of carnival as a crucial form of resistance that merges the political and the aesthetic. Inheriting from the innovative political approach of feminism and queer activism in the 1980s, and groups such as Reclaim the Streets! throughout the 1990s, rebel clowning is a form of political activism which aims to inject values often seen as distinct from the political realm: joy, pleasure, desire, diversity and horizontal power structures. The inspiration for such understanding of carnival is to be found notably in the theories of the Russian literary theorist Bakhtin (1984) and of the 1960s radical avant-garde known as the Situationists (Vaneigem, 1967). For both:

> [c]arnival was . . . a unitary 'world' of social relations that were independent and distinct from those of everyday life. These relations were characterized by the inversion of hierarchical relationships where the low mocked the high and all dogmas and hierarchies were suspended
>
> (Grindon, 2004, p. 149)

Over the last decade many events have been organised to give rise to such joyful revolutionary moments: Reclaim the Streets! parties worldwide, actions by the Italian White Overalls or the Pink and Silver bloc in various global events against the symbols of global capitalism such as the World Trade Organisation or the Group of 8 (G8) (Seattle in 1999, Prague in 2000, Genoa in 2001) have been read as inspiring examples of such carnivalesque moments (Shepard, 2003; Grindon, 2004). In these, resistance to capitalism is carried out on the protesters' terms rather than on the authorities' terms. Such events mark a striking difference from traditional marches or political rallies, whose organisation characteristically allegorises political determination and class solidarity. Such forms emphasise the anonymous mass, and the extent of its power and seriousness is gauged by numbers: of members in the party or the trade union, of workers on strike, of participants in the march. This conventional approach to demonstrations is characterised by its expectedness: the itinerary of the march is identical year after year; the chants and slogans repeated *ad infinitum*; the behaviour of the participants is itself codified and unchangeable. What is illustrated in the streets is the view of a revolution brought about by discipline and regimented hierarchy, which thus mirrors the system it intends to overthrow.

On the other hand the carnival is about joyful disruption, unpredictability and spontaneity. It 'consecrates inventive freedom' and its spirit 'offers the chance to have a new outlook on the world to realize the relative nature of all that exists, and to enter a completely new order of things' (Bakhtin, 1984, p. 34). The power of the carnival lies in its capacity to immediately transform reality, as opposed to being a mere step towards tomorrow's revolution. It offers individuals a space to be what they want to be without restrictions, as '[i]n its immediacy carnival refuses the constant mediation and representations of capitalism' (Notes from Nowhere, 2003, p. 175). Rebel clowning, in its carnivalesque spirit, is located in the long tradition of political demands to be in control of one's life, to participate in the world with a frank immediacy and to fulfil a sensual desire to be in the world, free of all separation, hierarchy and bureaucracy (Plant, 1992). Rebel clowning, like carnival, is rooted in a blurring of the distinction between art and life. It creates forms that merge the two and propagates acts of cultural resistance that eschew representation in favour of radical social transformation and direct action. The carnivalesque protest is inspired by theorists such as the Situationists (Vaneigem, 1967) or Hakim Bey (1991, 1994) who emphasise the potential for culture to have a revolutionary dimension by insisting on the notions of immediacy, pleasure and play. It 'does not acknowledge any distinction between actors and spectators' (Bakhtin, 1984, p. 168) and in this lies its liberatory and subversive nature. The carnival transforms the political space itself.

> Carnival also means turning what we consider to be political on its head. Mention the word *politics* and many people will imagine a world filled with words, and debate, a sterile, pleasureless world of talking heads.

The pleasures of the body have been banished from the public sphere of politics and the excitement of the erotic pushed into the narrow private confines of the sexual realm. But carnival brings the body back to public space, not the perfect smooth bodies that promote consumption on billboards and magazines, not the manipulated plastic bodies of MTV and party political broadcasts, but the body of warm flesh, of blood and guts, organs and orifices

(Notes from Nowhere, 2003, p. 175)

Re-appropriating our 'docile bodies'

Feminist adult educators were instrumental in terms of addressing the value of embodied learning and knowing within the field of adult education and learning (e.g. Crowther, Martin & Shaw, 1999). By bringing the 'real' body back to the centre of the public space, through its clear disobedience of the disciplinarian rules that regiment the body, carnival frees the 'docile bodies' (Foucault, 1979, 1980) and disembodied knowledge (Crowther, Martin & Shaw, 1999) from their position of subjection and gives them back their power. As Foucault (1980) argues:

Discipline produces subjected and practiced bodies, 'docile bodies'. Discipline increases the forces of the body (in economic terms of utility) and diminishes these same forces (in political terms of obedi- ence). In short, it dissociates power from the body; on the one hand, it turns it into an 'aptitude', a 'capacity', which it seeks to increase; on the other hand, it reverses the course of the energy, the power that might result from it, and turns it into a relation of subjection

(Foucault, 1980, p. 182)

In the carnival the body no longer responds to such discipline. It actually reverses its logic: the body re-appropriates its political power by refusing to be reduced to a 'capacity' and demonstrating its ability to be a source of pleasure. As it invades the streets with colourful crowds of musicians and dancers, it ignores the conventional rules of discourse that impose a specific tone of voice and mannerism, that condition the appropriate behaviour and body language in certain spaces or situations (which stop us singing out loud in a shopping mall or dancing laughing in the middle of the street). The carnival *embodies* disobedience.

And of course the clown and the fool are central characters of the carnival – not the insipid clown of kids' parties, the marketing character co-opted by the corporate multinational, or the enclosed figure of the circus, but the trickster, healer, shaman who, since the beginning of time, has had a fundamental critical social function that heals and critiques through disruption. Clowns and tricksters are characterised by their liminal nature, they are part of and at the margins of their cultures, and can express the opposite of their cultures' expected norms (Christen, 1998).

> Clowns around the world hold these paradoxical roles as merrymakers, religious specialists, healers and frightening thieves (. . .) In addition, clowns and tricksters often take the role of social commentators. They embarrass people who have broken one of society's rules. They also mock those in power, such as government officials, priests, and ritual specialists. Their mockery is meant to highlight the abuse of power and the role that people can play in reclaiming that power
>
> (Christen, 1998, p. xiii)

Transgression and unpredictability

The rebel clown combines the naivety and willingness to please of the theatrical clown with the cunning and street-wisdom of the buffoon and the activist. S/he transgresses all boundaries, refuses all dichotomies: often neither a male nor a female, neither artist nor activist, clever nor stupid, mad nor sane, entertainment nor threat. Ignoring and consciously ignorant of these oppressive binary oppositions s/he claims the position of the 'other' with pride as s/he plays with and against categorisation.

The most basic transgression in rebel clowning is breaking what in theatrical terms is called the fourth wall – the division between performer and audience. The rebel clown dissolves this wall between resister and oppressor through communication – of jokes, silly stunts, beautiful choreography and acts of love.

Instead of merely confronting his/her oppressors, s/he acknowledges their physical presence and gives them respect as fellow human beings. This is a radical departure from the confrontation of demonstrators and authority and here are the beginnings of disruption of power relations. As such the clown is utterly subversive: through him/her the boundaries that give authority its power disappear; by making him/herself impossible to categorise s/he inhabits a place outside these power relations. In a way s/he becomes untouchable.

It is through such transgressions that the rebel clown expresses his/her unpredictability. The rebel clown ruptures the pattern of making demands and threats that can be blocked. Instead, she asks permission and offers the opportunity for collaboration; at first the collaboration is watching: having set themselves up in physical opposition to the clowns, the 'authorities' have become a captive audience and are complicit in the clown's actions. They are caught in the uncomfortable position of being coerced to be part of the 'show'. They are working with the clowns who are thus in a powerful position since the clown thrives on attention. This is most obvious when clowns are being searched by the police. Police and army strategy is built around predictability and knowing what the 'enemy' will do next – but how can the police know what will happen when they decide to strip-search a gaggle of rebel clowns? How can they know that half of them are likely to dissolve in hysterical giggles because they are ticklish while the other half have so many layers of

A member of the Clandestine Insurgent Rebel Clowning Army at the anti-G8 protests. Scotland, July 2005. (Photograph by Ian Teh, www.ianteh.com)

clothing on that it will take all day before they are down to their stripy underwear? Rebel clowns become to the authorities what the women of Greenham Common were to the American soldiers on the Greenham Common base: strange creatures that fall outside the established patterns of resistance (Feminism and Nonviolence Study Group, 1983).

The ever-unpredictable reaction and behaviour of the clown explode the rigid codes that regiment normal social relationships and circumnavigate the usual patterns of reactivity that characterise relations of authority. When confrontation is expected (by the police or the security guard of a corporate building for instance), the clown offers assistance in securing the building, thereby completely deflating the importance of both the building and the security forces. The clown may also offer a loving demeanour: in July 2005 as riot police line up in Edinburgh to protect the G8 from being disrupted, brandishing their shields as a clear sign of authority and power, a tiara-wearing clown kisses and draws smiley faces with her lipstick to accompany the traces of her lips on the transparent plastic built to intimidate and repress.

Rebel clowning turns the world of violent direct action on its head. It turns fear of authority and arrest into a game of tag or grandmothers' footsteps. The power of clowning lies in the fact that the audience simultaneously laughs at and identifies with the clown, who slips on a banana skin and falls. Where the audience is in a position of oppressor or authority (police or army, security force at a street action), they may laugh at the clown's failure, simultaneously experiencing relief that they themselves are not being humiliated. Yet they end up in a contradictory position – they can have contempt for the clown, but they 'fail' by their own standards because their usual tactics are rendered inefficient.

Instead of resisting, the clown collaborates; instead of obeying and hating, the rebel clown mocks and slips away. The ideology of civil disobedience and direct action is creatively interpreted and implemented. As the police attempt to control crowd movements by ordering protesters to stay behind a line on the road, the rebel clowns obsessively want to know what is so special with the line in question . . . so much so that the officers no longer dare mention the line, deeply affecting the power relation between the two 'camps'. The humour and laughter that characterises the clown are thus profoundly subversive. As Kolonel Klepto, one of the fictional spokespersons of CIRCA, says:

We dismantle their power through the liberating force of laughter and like the body of the clown laughter is slippery and ever changing. You can laugh *at* someone and *with* someone, one minute it's an act of solidarity, the next a gesture of contempt. Like fear – the force that those in power try to control us with – laughter is infectious. Where fear constricts and closes, laughter releases. It opens the body and mind, throwing it into a transformative chaos – it can turn humiliation into humour and a situation of terror into revealer of truth. It's a form of sensuous solidarity which criss-crosses the normal lines of conflict – one minute those in authority are laughing at your stupidity, the next they are cowering from the mockery targeted at them

(Klepto, 2004, p. 410)

Rebel clown training

In order to share and extend the rebel clown practice we devised a 'basic training'. This consisted of a series of activities organised over two days, and provided an introduction to different elements of rebel clowning: Spontaneity, Play, Presence, *Complicité, Bouffon.*

Rebel clown training doesn't pretend to make participants into clowns over two days. This art requires many years and immense commitment. Rather it is an introduction to a new way of being and thinking. The entire training event aims to be a transformational learning experience, a personal liberation through a collective endeavour. During the training, we access our own creativity and imagination and find ways to start freeing ourselves from the conditioning to behave in ways which serves the neo-liberal project. As trainers we do not see ourselves as separate from the trainees. We do not transfer our expertise but rather, as co-participants, we share views and experience. Critical reflection there-fore plays an important part in the training: each activity is discussed before going onto the next one. These discussions are crucial to empha-sise the multi-layered nature of rebel clowning, especially its possible applications to many different situations, including direct actions (i.e. potentially confrontational situations). We also explore the process of collective working practices, especially the intertwined relationship between individuality and collectivity.

Importantly, desire and play are at the forefront of the educational experience, as is the recognition of the 'potential for empowerment through learning about pleasure' (Barr, 1999, p. 116).

The training practice has been influenced by critical pedagogy, feminist adult educators and action researchers involved in the devising of the rebel clowning practice. They see themselves as critical educators because 'critical educators have to help the oppressed overcome a "culture of silence" in which they cannot see that their situation could be different and that they could intervene to transform it' (Barr, 1999, p. 15).

Rebel clown training aims to develop creative tools based on play and pleasure, in order to explore issues of oppression, inhibitions, self-censorship and ways to address them in an empowering fashion. From the beginning we create a space using the words 'game' and 'exercise' interchangeably to accustom participants to the idea that work can be synonymous with play and that games can be serious. Deceptively simple games demonstrate that one learns as much with one's own body as with one's mind (hooks, 1994a; Feldenkrais, 1987) and also draw attention to the amount of knowledge that can be released through pleasure, emotions and imagination. This is a crucial dimension of radical adult education, which promotes 'new meanings and knowledge rather than simply increasing access to existing knowledge' (Barr, 1999, p. 17).

For instance, the Name Switch game consists of alternating two actions: firstly participants point at and name objects as they walk around the room, then they point at the same objects and call them what they are not (e.g. pointing at a table and calling it "sky"). We speed up the process of alternating between the two actions (usual name/other name) to continually disrupt the process of logical thinking and encourage spontaneity, one of the keys to the clown's unpredictability. This activity encourages discussion of the extent to which we are all conditioned into thinking in very set ways. Sharing our experience, we can critically reflect on the pervasive (self-) discipline which rules our lives and discuss what we want to do about it.

These notions are also explored through Hug Tag, where participants have to hug someone in order not be 'tagged'. It allows us to rediscover the pleasurable and healing power of touch, freed from rigid societal rules, which strictly codify and limit touch to specific realms such as the sexual, the medical, the sportive. This emphasis re-acquaints participants with their own bodies, to break away from their 'docile bodies' (Foucault, 1979, 1980). Here again play has a subversive dimension: it breaks down the rigid conditioning of compartmentalised body uses in public spaces.

This game is also crucial in breaking the established pattern of running away in the face of apparent danger as the priority is to rescue one's fellow clowns by hugging them. In this game the more we run away the more likely we are to be caught. A reflective discussion invariably leads to an analysis of crowd behaviour, of one's innate strategic ability to move and react to others, or of the importance of collective responsibility for one another in a difficult situation (e.g. avoiding one's own and others' arrest during a civil disobedience action). It emphasises the participants' embodied knowledge, by demonstrating how we already know how to react in such situations, albeit in an unconscious way.

Subjugated knowledges

Rebel clown training is rooted in a view of education:

> ... which rests on the development of new knowledge through dialogue and the collective sharing and analysing of experience. The kind of educational practice based on that view of knowledge recognizes and takes seriously – concretely not just in theory – both the emotional component of learning and knowledge and the social and political interests that invest it ...
>
> (Barr, 1999, p. 24)

Thus rebel clowning aims to tap into subjugated knowledges, the knowledges buried under dominant discourses (Foucault, 1980), common knowledge, intuitions, knowledge 'from below', springing from emotions, imagination. The training counters the dominant tendency by which 'knowledge arising out of the ability to work with people, with emotions, with a range of modes of thinking is devalued as subjective knowledge' (Barr, 1999, p. 112). As mentioned above many activities focus on the power of imagination and emotions to explore important issues related to oppression and to provide ourselves and each other with the confidence to address them. We indeed acknowledge the complex, often contradictory nature, of oppression (in that we are all at once oppressed and oppressor at some level) and believe that 'the development of critical self-understanding on the part of those "below" is a weapon against it' (Barr, 1999, p. 15). The ways in which we address the issues of hierarchy and (self-) coercion are a creative approach to this development.

Indeed rebel clowning is clearly located in a non-authoritarian and non-hierarchical framework. It demonstrates that social relationships can be functional and fulfilling beyond and without hierarchy. Therefore, as well as introducing the principles of consensus decision-making, the training includes activities based on the notion of 'emergent intelligence' which demonstrate that a group with no single leader can act and respond.

Fishing is a particularly powerful example of this approach: we form groups of five to 15 people, all facing the same way. We give the example of a shoal of fish which seems to change direction with a different leader at each turn without a discussion. The person at the head of the group or shoal starts to move forward slowly while the whole shoal follows. The head of the group must ensure that the shoal remains together – so s/he must be aware of the speed with which s/he moves and the capacity of the rest of the group to follow. A change of direction must be initiated by the head of the group at that time. As s/he stops and takes a 90 degree turn to the left or right another person is at the head of the group, and s/he starts to move.

As the game progresses we all become used to one another's ways of moving and rhythms so the movement and changing of 'leaders' becomes more fluid and less obvious. A collective choreography, built on each previous movement/sound/rhythm, begins to emerge. Participants realise that decisions can be made by following the emergent intelligence of the group, without the need for one particular leader. This activity emphasises the importance of collective commitment and responsibility for this to function. Fishing encourages participants who tend to refuse/evade initiative to take responsibility and act. It also highlights those who do not like to give up leadership in a very concrete yet subtle way.

With the activity Yes, Let's All . . . we explore ways of disrupting established patterns of reaction and response from authority/resisters. One participant begins by suggesting an action (e.g. Let's all pick flowers), all must then respond by repeating the idea (e.g. Yes! Let's all pick flowers!) and mimicking the action. After a certain amount of time, someone else comes up with a different idea and the pattern repeats. In

Not only a game: Rebel clowns go "Fishing" at the anti-G8 protests. Scotland, July 2005. (Photograph by Ian Teh, www.ianteh.com)

collaborating with what we might think is a ridiculous idea, we go against our instinct to self-censor and censor the other, thereby losing some of our inhibitions and going beyond the limits of our own imagination. As well as using the ruptures in behaviour to establish new ways of perceiving and working, Yes, Let's All . . . encourages participants to surrender their egos and be open to others' ideas and desires.

This willingness to surrender can shortcut discussion and division on the streets when a quick consensus decision is needed. Yes, Let's All . . . also reveals the different rhythms which exist in a group: some people jump in with their own idea before the first proposal has had time to take root, others will never initiate an action. A reflective discussion provides an opportunity for the group to discuss the effects of different timings – for effective group actions on the streets, for our personal rhythms, in order to create trust in a group.

The notion of trust is particularly important in networked and non-hierarchical structures as the sustainability of such structures depends on all members' commitment to its functioning; there is no authority to refer to which can force anyone to do anything they do not want to do. Establishing networks of support and solidarity to advance social justice is a clear purpose of radical adult education (Crowther, Martin & Shaw, 1999) and rebel clown training encourages this. We unashamedly stress the importance of love as a learning tool for critical self-understanding and we explore this with the notion of Presence and more specifically the pleasure of being present: Pass The Red Nose has participants singing an uplifting song whilst passing a red nose around the group. When the facilitator shouts "Stop!" the group steps back and the participant who has the red nose holds it aloft with great pride and pleasure. S/he then puts it on and stands in front of the group motionless and silent but being happy to be there, to be looked at and appreciated. The clown attempts to do nothing while the facilitator compliments him/her on his/her hair, eyes, ears, smile, whilst the entire group watches with love and support. The process repeats until all participants have worn the red nose.

This activity enables us to become conscious of the physical and emotional self we present in public and to adjust that to different situations so that we can work confidently without embarrassment in the specific space of spectator–performer, applied to other situations (e.g. the street). More importantly it instils pleasure and confidence in being in the world (including confrontational situations), and in standing up for our beliefs. This pleasure and confidence is encouraged greatly by trust and support from people around us.

Following bell hooks' notion that love is making the other free to be what they want to be (1994b) a simple activity such as Pass The Red Nose, shows the importance of collective responsibility for each individual feeling valued, loved and thus able to trust. Such confidence paves the way to greater charisma and releasing of the imagination which is infectious and self-sustaining. This in turn leads to a feeling for the potential for change and justice through collective action.

Conclusion

As the feminist Audre Lorde points out, we have the capacity to challenge our own ways of feeling and emotion – as well as knowing – through collective inquiry. She questions the depth of critical understanding of the forces that shape our lives that can be achieved if we use only the rational and abstract methods of analysis. As the parable says 'the master's tools will never dismantle the master's house' (in Barr, 1999, p. 114).

Rebel clowning is an exploration of such collective enquiry whilst encouraging personal transformation and healing. As we explore our relationship to coercion, self-censorship, (self-) discipline and authoritarianism, we collectively engage in challenging the structures of oppression which affect our lives. As this is carried out through play, we rediscover the pleasure to learn and the power of imagination and emotions as weapons against domination. Rebel clowning offers a process rather than solutions or a system. It leaves us free to imagine, question and continually strive for development and transformation towards social justice.

References

Anon. (1997) Reclaim the streets! *Do or die: Voices from the ecological resistance.* Issue 6, pp. 1–10.

Bakhtin, M. (1984) *Rabelais and his world.* Bloomington: Indiana University Press.

Barr, J. (1999) *Liberating knowledge. Research, feminism and adult education.* Leicester: NIACE.

Bey, H. (1991) *Temporary autonomous zones.* New York: Autonomedia.

Bey, H. (1994) *Immediatism.* Oakland, CA: AK Press.

Carr, W. and Kemmis, S. (1986) *Becoming critical: Education, knowledge and action research.* Lewes: Falmer.

Christen, K. (1998) *Clowns and tricksters. An encyclopedia of culture and tradition.* Denver: ABC-CLIO.

Crowther, J., Martin, I. and Shaw, M. (1999) *Popular education and social movements in Scotland today.* Leicester: NIACE.

Feldenkrais, M. (1987) *Awareness through movement, health exercises for personal growth.* London: Penguin.

Feminism and Nonviolence Study Group (1983) *Piecing it together.* United Kingdom: The Feminism and Nonviolence Study Group.

Foucault, M. (1979) *Discipline and punish.* New York: Vintage Books.

Foucault, M. (1980) *Power/Knowledge. Selected interviews and other writings,* 1972–1977. (ed) Colin Gordon, New York: Pantheon Press.

Grindon, G. (2004) 'Carnival against capital: a comparison of Bakhtin, Vaneigem and Bey.' *Anarchist Studies,* Vol. 12, No. 2, pp. 146–61.

hooks, b. (1994a) *Teaching to transgress.* London: Routledge.

hooks, b. (1994b) *Outlaw culture: Resisting representations.* New York: Routledge.

Klein, N. (2002) *Fences and windows.* London: Flamingo.

Klepto, K. (2004) 'Making war with love: the Clandestine Insurgent Rebel Clown Army,' *City,* Vol. 8, No. 3, pp. 403–11.

McTaggart, R. (1996) 'Issues for participatory action researchers.' In O. Zuber-Skerritt (ed), *New Directions in Action Research.* London: Falmer Press.

Notes from Nowhere (2003) *We are everywhere. The irresistible rise of global anti-capitalism.* London: Verso.

Plant, S. (1992) *The most radical gesture. The Situationist International in a post-modern age.* London: Routledge.

Reclaim the Streets! (1996) *Untitled agit-prop.* Great Britain: Reclaim the Streets!

Shepard, B. (2003) 'Absurd responses vs. earnest politics; Global justice vs. anti-war movements; Guerilla Theater and Aesthetic Solutions'. *The Journal of Aesthetics and Protest,* Vol. 1, No. 2 http://www.journalof aestheticsandprotest.org/1/BenShepard/index.html

Vaneigem, R. (1967) *Traité de savoir vivre à l'usage des jeunes générations,* Paris: Gallimard.

CHAPTER 2

Educating socially-responsive practitioners

What can the literary arts offer health-professional education?

Elizabeth Anne Kinsella

Introduction

I have discovered that literature (for me) has the potential of making visible what has sunk out of sight, of restoring a lost vision and a lost spontaneity.

Maxine Greene (1995, p. 77)

Artistic and literary approaches to health professional education and training have tended to be at best haphazard, and at worst marginalised (Darbyshire, 1995). Indeed, like so many practices for social justice, Darbyshire (1995) characterises the practice of using literary texts to educate health care practitioners as subversive. I wonder if this 'subversive' label reflects the potential of the literary arts to challenge conventional approaches to health care education and practice. Rather than a traditional focus on scientific, technical, empirical, and measurable information, literature has the potential to draw attention to what occurs in the feeling structure, mind, imagination, and sensibility of living social beings (Greene, 1991). In this way the literary arts may offer a stimulus to moral imagination (Evans, Greaves & Pickering, 1997) and practitioner consciousness (Downie, 1999) within health care practice.

Indeed, many scholars have noted the capacity of narrative accounts to awaken a variety of sensibilities in health professionals. For instance, narrative accounts may encourage practitioners to realise a greater range of responses in clinical and moral decision-making (Nisker, 2004), to become more compassionate (Nisker, 2001), to become sensitised to ethical uses of power (Kinsella, 2005), to consider alternative represent-ations and interpretations of disability or illness experiences (Kleinman, 1995, 1988) and to learn how others cope in the face of disappointment or illness (Frank, 1995; Gillon, 1997; Wendell, 1996). They may also assist practitioners to consider diversity (Parsons, 2004), to become attuned to caring behaviours (Noddings, 1995; Wright St. Clair, 2001), to engage the moral imagination (Nussbaum, 1990; Scott, 1997) and to consider different ways of understanding suffering and illness (Garro & Mattingly, 2000; Nelson, 2001, Kleinman, 1988, 1995). Such insights are highly relevant to the preparation of socially-responsive health professionals, concerned with compassion and justice in health care settings, and add to the approaches available to practitioners in meeting the needs of their patients.

In the interests of promoting socially just practices, I suggest that it is time to reconsider the role of the literary arts in the preparation of health professionals, and the design of healthcare curricula. Travelling this terrain begins to tease out creative ways in which the arts can contribute to the preparation of responsive, socially-aware healthcare practitioners. Despite Darbyshire's (1995) lament about the marginalisation of this practice it appears that growing numbers of educators identify literature as a heuristic for the preparation of health services professions (Coles, 1989; Downie, 1999; Gold, 1991). Nisker (2004) provides an eloquent summary of why this may be the case:

> Stories, whether true, fictional, or fictional based on truth, can help bring the reader or audience to the position of the person requiring health care, thus allowing a much deeper appreciation of that person's needs, rights, and desires than is possible in health care and philosophy tomes. By approximating empathy for the person at the centre of the decision-making, ethics explorers and educators can better contribute to moral resolution of the issue at hand, and provide better care (pp. 291–2).

In this chapter I explore how the literary arts can foster learning and be used to help those being trained and educated as health professionals to move toward a deeper appreciation of social justice agendas within health care. In particular, I focus on my own learning and what the literary arts have brought to me. Nisker (2004) has pointed out that for fictional works to contribute to moral exploration in health care practice 'it is not necessary that they describe medical moments, health care settings, or illness experiences . . . [rather] it is necessary, that they power-fully surface the feelings of the persons involved and explore humanness in a manner that can be absorbed for later understanding' (p. 286). Van Manen (2002) concurs. Illuminating the power of the narrative text, he writes: 'There is something paradoxical about the unreality of a powerful text: it can be experienced by the writer or reader as real, as unreally real, as nearer than the nearness that things may have in ordinary reality' (p. 7). He goes on to write:

> Many readers have at one time or another been profoundly moved in the realization of being touched by a human insight. And this insight might not have affected us this deeply if we had undergone the experience in the sober light of day, rather than in the realm of the novel, story, or poem. (p. 7)

Thus, the conception of literary arts that I adopt in this chapter includes texts that may or may not be directly situated in healthcare practice. Rather, the focus is on texts that foster moral exploration and awareness about social and relational issues. Different texts are interpreted in distinct ways by different individuals, and the same text may have both distinct and similar meanings for individuals (Lesser, 2002; Sumara, 1996). Therefore, literary art is defined here in the broadest sense as literary fiction, narrative, stories, and testimonials, and these terms are used interchangeably throughout this chapter.

The literary arts in health professional education

In this examination of the literary arts in health professional education, I propose five interrelated themes that illuminate how engagement with literary art may influence learning. These include: new ways of seeing, grasping new meanings, changes in consciousness, transformative dimensions, and praxis. These themes are arbitrarily separated from one another in this discussion; in actuality they overlap and are interwoven. Examples from my own experience and those reported by other authors are highlighted throughout.

New ways of seeing

Art breaks open a dimension inaccessible to other experience, a dimension:

> . . . in which human beings, nature, and things no longer stand under the law of the established reality principle . . . The encounter with the truth of art happens in the estranging language and images which make perceptible, visible, audible that which is no longer or not yet perceived, said, and heard in everyday life.
>
> (Marcuse, 1978, p. 72)

Marcuse suggests that art breaks open new ways of perceiving, by tapping into a dimension inaccessible to other experience. If his words are true, then literature and story, particularly accessible art forms, have the potential to foster new ways of seeing.

Many educators in healthcare have broadened their approaches to teaching in order to raise awareness of multiple ways of understanding the worlds of health practitioners, patients, the concepts of health, illness, disability, as well as the health care and sociopolitical systems in which health practitioners work (Darbyshire, 1995). Darbyshire suggests that narrative texts offer tremendous potential as sites to foster dialogue about important issues in the health professions. Furthermore, the study of narratives can reveal multiple interpretations and allow for exploration of textual and wider professional issues from a variety of perspectives. In this way, the study of narratives can be seen as a means to expand the interpretive frames of health professionals and as a means to explore professional issues from a broad range of perspectives.

Robert Coles (1989), a professor of medicine at Harvard University, suggests that literature can provide a means of moral and social inquiry. He teaches courses entitled *Literature and medicine* and *A literature of social reflection*. He notes that teaching through literature constantly reminds him of how complex, ironic, ambiguous and fateful life can be, and that the conceptual categories that he learned in psychiatry, in psycho-analysis, and in social science seminars, are not the only means by which one might view the world (p. xvii). Similarly, Maxine Greene notes that 'each time a reader engages a novel, it will change; she or he can neither exhaust nor completely realise it' (1991, p. 265). She goes on to say that 'this is in tune with the perspectival nature of knowing' and, with what she calls the 'enticing incompleteness of the world' (Greene, 1991, p. 265).

At a time when medicine seems to have gained an unprecedented cognitive and social authority (Wendell, 1996) – in the sense that health professionals have considerable authority to name what is taken seriously and believed to be real in healthcare environments (Kinsella, 2005) – I suggest that education that promotes awareness of life's ambiguity and contextuality (Lyotard, 1979; Schön, 1983), as opposed to a false sense of certainty, is desirable for health professionals. Furthermore, an education that helps practitioners to recognise the partiality of their knowledge (Greene, 1988; Simon, 1992), as opposed to infusing a false sense of one 'fixed' view of the world, seems to me to be an important and overlooked consideration in how we prepare health professionals for practice. Such an approach might be viewed as a pedagogy of possibility as it provokes new ways of seeing by providing a location where critique can safely be carried out. It

> . . . might be thought of as a counter-discursive activity that attempts to provoke a process through which people might engage in a trans-formative critique of their everyday lives. This means addressing the naturalness of dominant ways of seeing, saying, and doing by provoking a consideration of why things are the way they are, how they got to be that way, in what ways might change be desirable, and what it would take for things to be otherwise.
>
> (Simon, 1992, p. 60)

As an example, I recently read a work of fiction entitled *Cereus Blooms at Night* (Mootoo, 1998), which caused me to think about the notion of 'care' in new ways. Sometimes it seems that the systems in healthcare work against our efforts to care for our clients. Our good intentions may be overruled by systemic factors that can oppress both the healthcare worker and the client (Townsend, 1998; Campo, 1997). I see this theme taken up in *Cereus Blooms at Night*. The book is a narrative of Mala Ramchandin's life as told through the eyes of a male nurse, Tyler. In this story, Tyler shows courage and responsiveness, as he unearths questions for the reader about what it means to 'care'. Early in the story Tyler speaks of his sense of powerlessness in the face of an authoritarian nun, the administrator of the nursing home in which he works:

> Sister again shrieked and ordered me to deposit Miss Ramchandin on the bed, which had not yet been made, and to strap her down again. I hardly had opened my mouth to explain that Miss Ramchandin was too frail to inflict even a bad thought when Sister screamed at me for being insolent and blatantly disregarding her authority. I placed Miss Ramchandin on the bed yet still hesitated to get the straps. Sister scuttled out into the yard and came back shortly with a length of rope from Mr. Hector. I raced back to the office, yanked the straps off the stretcher and returned in time to contain Miss Ranchandin myself. I made a production of pulling at the straps but in truth only loosely buckled them. Faced with the threat of losing my job, I agreed not to unbind her again.
>
> (Mootoo, 1998, p. 13)

Freire (1989) suggests that naming an oppressive situation is the first step in overcoming it. Perhaps reading a passage such as this has the potential to help us to name our experience and to change the way we see it. As I read this passage, I am reminded of the moral complexity of professional practice. Although this is an extreme example, it demonstrates a phenomenon that can occur in many subtle forms in practice. Faced with losing one's job or 'toeing the line', it is sometimes difficult for health professionals to speak up about unfair or uncaring practices in the workplace. I suggest that reading a passage like the one above has the potential to heighten one's awareness of power relations in the workplace, and to raise questions about the morality of such practices. Furthermore, it can raise awareness of the hegemony of certain work environments and the potential for actions to be co-opted by unjust managerial practices.

Later in the story Tyler resists the oppression. In his anger he unties Miss Ramchandin's straps:

Tears streamed down her face and her body was contorted. Fuelled by outrage I undid the straps around her feet. Then I unfastened the ones around her thighs and across her chest. She continued to cry as if unaware of my presence, and her body slowly tightened even more into the contortion the straps had temporarily curtailed. I sat by her head, slipped my arm under her back and pulled her into my arms. I held her against my chest, rocking her until the first streaks of morning light broke through the pitch black sky. She had by this time fallen asleep, her head leaning on my chest.

(Mootoo, 1998, p. 22)

I am reminded here of words from Marge Piercy's poem *A just anger:* 'A good anger acted upon is beautiful as lightning and swift with power. A good anger swallowed, a good anger swallowed clots of blood to slime' (Sewell, 1991, p. 173). In this example Tyler is swift with power; he takes courageous action toward caring, transfiguring himself. He resists orders to strap Mala, and he resists the traditional model of health care which would see 'holding a client' and being 'vulnerable' with that client as 'unprofessional'.

Maxine Greene (1991) suggests that literature can change the way we see by presenting unsettling images that fuel a reaction from the reader. 'Outrage may flood in . . . that is when, with images of the lost and violated imbued with indignation, readers may see themselves acting to stop such things, to mend a wound in human existence that never seems to heal' (p. 259). Reading passages such as the ones above invites one to see in new ways, and to foster difficult questions of ourselves such as 'what would I have done in this situation?' I suggest that including quotes or readings of this nature in courses that prepare health practitioners for practice have unexplored potential. For instance, when I teach ethics to students in occupational therapy, they often write in their journals about the ethical tensions they experience around the use of restraints in nursing homes and hospitals. Invoking a literary quote such as the one above serves to foster an engaged dialogue on various issues with respect to decision making about the use of restraints. Furthermore, students often write of feeling constrained within prescribed roles and traditions, and of feeling powerless as students to act on their moral inclinations. Reading and discussing quotes from literary texts provides a way to explore such issues from a safe distance, and can foster dialogue about broader issues of power and empowerment, and human rights (both practitioner and patient rights) within health care environments.

As I read these passages I see some of the subtle inner conflicts that I have experienced in practice illuminated in the drama. It is the conflict between systemic regulations and an inner call (Kinsella, 2006), the call that Noddings (1995) refers to as the 'call to care'. Roach (1998) writes that 'caring is humankind at home, being real, being myself, being yourself . . . To the extent that I am uncaring: to that extent am I less than human' (p. 31). Although an extreme example, reading these passages has helped me to see more clearly a particular tension that permeated my professional practice in healthcare, the tension between the inner call to care, and the systemic factors that at times overrule my 'good intentions' in this regard.

I suggest that literary fiction, with its ability to represent the way certain events, if they had happened, may have unfolded (Carr, 1986, p. 13), is one means of fostering new ways of seeing. Such a re-visioning could benefit health professionals by broadening the perspectives and viewpoints from which we view the worlds of our practices, and by helping us to find the frames to critique our practices and envision new possibilities.

Grasping new meanings

> The only way into a piece of literature is through the front door – Open It. Once there, if the arrangement of the room is unfamiliar and the fabric strange, reflect that at least it is new, and that is what you say you want. It will be too, a world apart, a place where the normal weights and measures of a day have been subtly altered to give a different emphasis and perhaps to slide back the secret panel by the heart.
>
> (Winterson, 1995, p. 43)

These words by Winterson speak to one of the potentials of literature. Literature offers the possibility of making strange that which was familiar, of gently opening our hearts to different meanings than the ones that we have previously attached ourselves to.

Bruner (1986) notes that although stories are about events in a 'real' world, 'they render that world newly strange, rescue it from obviousness, fill it with gaps' in such a way that the reader is called upon to compose a virtual text in response. If we ask about the reader's conception of what kind of story or text s/he is encountering or recreating, we are asking a question about the interpretive processes that are loosed in the reader's mind (Bruner, 1986), a question about meaning. Through literature the reader actively engages with different ways of interpreting events, of attributing meanings to events whose meanings may have become taken-for-granted. Iser (1989) suggests 'that meanings in literary texts are generated in the act of reading; they are the product of a complex inter-action between the text and the reader, and not qualities that are hidden in the text' (p. 5). The reader, working in collaboration with the writer, creates patterns in her or his experience, discovers meanings scarcely suspected before (Greene, 1991).

One book that I vividly remember opening new meanings for me was *Anna Karenina* by Leo Tolstoy (1954). I read it shortly after I graduated from high school. At the time I had a narrow view of divorce. As I entered the world of Anna Karenina through Tolstoy's words, my simplistic black and white ideas were challenged. I wrestled with Anna through her dilemma of what to do in the face of passionate love presenting itself outside of an oppressive marriage. In this story the stigma of divorce, the inability of the two lovers to build a respectable life together ends in tragedy. After I read this book the meaning of divorce was transformed for me. My moralistic frame came crashing apart, and was restructured into a new more open and understanding perspective. I could see how the stigma of divorce was hurtful. Further-more, I began to understand and empathise with what the lived experience of divorce must be, and the inner turmoil that accompanies it. While this example is not directly relevant to healthcare, I offer it as an example of how a work of fiction can change the way we make meaning, and potentially increase our compassion, our sense of empathy, our willingness to see from another perspective. Often healthcare prac-titioners have so much scientific content to learn and to remain current with, that the notion of entering the lifeworld of the client is not highlighted as a priority. I suggest that reading a book like *Anna Karenina* reminds one of the inner life, the passions and also — given the tragic nature of the end of the book — the contradictions, the social stigmas, and how these relational dimensions influence mental health and the will to live. One might ask "Was Anna Karenina healthy?" "How did society's reaction to her relationships contribute to or detract from her mental health?" "How do social issues and stigma potentially influence quality of life?"

Thus, reading literary fiction involves the reader in an interpretive act that can foster awareness of meanings that differ from one's own. By rendering what was familiar strange, reading literature and stories has the potential to foster changes in the meanings that individuals attribute to previously taken-for-granted situations. In fact, certain novels have the potential to estrange readers from the normal or the taken-for-granted, sometimes for years of their lives (Greene, 1991), or as in my experience, sometimes forever. This is particularly important in health education and care, where practitioners construct meanings about what the client has to say. Health practitioners frequently adopt authority in the stories they construct about the people they work with and these stories have moral import (Kinsella, 2005). I suggest that engagement with literary arts can reawaken attention to the lived experience of those with whom we work, and draw attention to the ethical imperative to co-construct meaning with our clients in concert with their stories, rather than to impose our meanings unilaterally upon them (Kinsella, 2005).

Changes in consciousness

> We have come to recognize that aware engagements with literary art –
> that the use of imagination those engagements make possible – make a
> great deal happen in human consciousness
>
> (Greene, 1991, p. 253)

Maxine Greene (1991, 1995) suggests that aware engagement with literature has the potential to change human consciousness. She writes of the unique capabilities of literature in this regard: 'remembered literary encounters can open pathways in one's mind and experience that no other articulations can open in the same way' (Greene, 1995, p. 78).

Paulo Freire (1989) has written that education either submerges consciousness by anaesthetising the individual and inhibiting creative power, or it strives for the emergence of consciousness through a constant unveiling of reality. Active engagement with literature can provide one means for fostering growth of consciousness.

For example, Christine Jarvis (1999), through her study, found that critically reading popular romantic fiction with adult women in the United Kingdom fostered changes in perspectives, and changes in consciousness about women's roles. Jarvis' (1999) study revealed that critically reflecting on popular fiction has the potential to foster critical thinking by encouraging individuals to:

> probe their habitual ways of thinking and acting (and those of others around them) for their underlying assumptions — those taken-for-granted values, common-sense ideas, and stereotypical notions about human nature and social organization that underlie our actions
>
> (Brookfield, 1987, p. 15–16, cited in Jarvis, 1999, p. 123)

One of the women in the study, Delia, reflected on the change that occurred in her thinking: 'Um, before, I used to think that we're all here to get married, stay at home, look after our husbands and children, but I don't think that it has to be like that. I think we should be independent' (p. 120).

Maxine Greene (1988) suggests that, in educational projects, critiques must be developed that uncover what masquerade as neutral frameworks in our everyday lives. Literature can foster this process, by helping us to look critically at what Greene calls the 'cloud of givenness' (1995, p. 47) or what Freire (1989) calls the 'circle of certainty' (p. 23). Greene (1991) reflects that a critical process unfolds naturally, when intentional activity is brought to bear upon literature: 'If readers can remain aware of what they are doing, if they can watch themselves being involved even as they are involved, they cannot but feel the critical questions arise' (p. 257).

By bringing questions to that which has been taken-for-granted, the consciousness of the individual can be raised. Literature that provokes indignation as it unveils injustice or brings attention to what was previously hidden can be particularly powerful:

> If literature has the capacity, however, to engage readers in such a manner as now and then to appeal to their indignation (because of the impact of the discourse, the language, or the enactments), those readers' lives might well be changed. They might at least be able to see, to attend, and to notice what was hidden until then. Attending, they might discern faultlines, deviations, gaps that might call upon them to reject withdrawal and choose some sort of action, to surpass
>
> (Greene, 1991, p. 261)

Thus, aware engagement with literature offers the possibilities of the emergence of consciousness, as opposed to its submergence. I suggest that healthcare practitioners who are more aware, and whose creative power has emerged will be better able to identify and work toward social justice agendas. While scientific knowledge is necessary, I suggest that more attention to the inner lives, the human dimensions, and the taken-for-granted social, political, economic, discursive and cultural dimensions is warranted in health professional education. Well-chosen literary texts can complement the education of health professionals by fostering the emergence of conscious awareness about a range of such issues pertinent to practice.

Transformative dimensions

Engagement with a piece of literature has the potential to change our very being, to transform who we are. As Jeanette Winterson (1995) writes:

> The book does not reproduce me, it re-defines me, pushes at my boundaries, shatters the palings that guard my heart. Strong texts work along the borders of our minds and alter what already exists (p. 26).

Winterson's words eloquently capture the possibility that exists for each of us to move to new locations, to redefine our own boundaries, as we read a text.

Sumara (1998) identifies the act of reading literary fiction as participation in a continual reorganisation of one's identity. Iser (1989) suggests that central to the reading of every literary work is the interaction between the structure of the text and its recipient. In looking at how such an interaction might work, Beach (1998) notes that when students engage with a text they often begin by applying certain preconceptions, often stereotypical, only to discover that these conceptions are contradicted by the particulars of the text world. Maxine Greene (1991) elaborates:

> A narrative given unexpected solidity by referring to materials summoned up from the reader's past, what has been comfortable and familiar, may suddenly be defamiliarized. Certain aspects of the reader's lived biography will emerge as figures against a ground – aspects never

heeded before: childhood racism and superstitions, perhaps; powerlessness in a dehumanized world; the ambiguities of the "natural man" and of nature itself; the distortion in a womanless space (p. 257).

Such a contradiction, between the reader's past experience and preconceptions and the new material presented in a text, fuels an internal dialogue in which beliefs, attitudes, and constructions of the world can undergo shifts. The text therefore interacts with the subjectivity of the reader. This interaction can challenge previously-held assumptions, and previous ways of being in the world, and therefore can foster what Mezirow (1991) calls a perspective transformation. As one's perspectives change, so one's identity shifts, and the individual is transformed. Mezirow (1991) sees perspective transformation as a continual process of development in adulthood.

Phillip Darbyshire (1995) teaches a course entitled *Understanding caring through arts and humanities* in the department of nursing and community health at Glasgow Caledonian University. This course is framed largely around the reading of, and reflection upon narratives. Darbyshire (1995) notes that a number of students spoke about how the course changed them in very personal ways. One student reported: 'this is the first course that was unusual in the respect that it made me think more of the way I am as a person rather than just what I do for my job' (p. 214). While another student said, 'I doubt if anything's left unchanged. Every piece of work I'm presented with has changed me bit by bit. I didn't think I was capable in some cases of changing' (p. 214).

A view of literature as in relationship with the reader, contrasts a traditional notion that literature merely provides vicarious experience or entertainment, escape, or moral lessons for the reader (Lesser, 2002; Sumara, 1998). Sumara (1998) suggests that in considering the relationship between the reader's identity and the reader's knowledge, the act of reading ought to be considered as an important site for the contestation and negotiation of already slippery and shifting identities. Thus, the relationship between the reader and the literature has transformative potential. This is important in health professional education if one recognises that actions are informed by the views that one holds about the world – in other words personal and professional transformations influence behaviours in practice. Darbyshire's course, *Understanding caring through arts and humanities*, provides an example of a transformative teaching practice that promotes social justice through the recognition of clients' narratives and through the cultivation of an ethics of care in health care practice.

Praxis

Praxis represents the place where reflection and action meet within the individual (Freire, 1989). Praxis is a dynamic coming together of these apparent dichotomies. When we take praxis to our workplace, we are acting out of an informed consciousness. The importance of praxis in professional practice has been highlighted by Donald Schön (1983, 1987) who has coined the phrase 'reflective practice'. This short phrase 'reflective practice' brings together the two dimensions of praxis within it: 'reflection' and 'practice' or 'action'. Schön (1983, 1987) suggests that in order to be effective in professional practice we need to reflect on our actions – in the midst of practice and retrospectively. I suggest that the literary arts can help practitioners in this task of reflecting on what is currently occurring and what has occurred in past practice.

For instance, a number of years ago, I read Oliver Sacks' book, *The man who mistook his wife for a hat*. Reflection on this book changed actions and my way of being in practice. The book was a collection of stories about people with a range of neurological conditions. Sacks' book awakened new possibilities and sensitivities in me through these stories. As a reader I felt that my vision and understanding of the experience of various neurological conditions and the implications for everyday life greatly expanded. Sacks' recognition of the 'human being' beyond the 'condition' was a refreshing frame through which to view my clients, and was an important complement to the 'clinical' frame of my training. Thus the stories fuelled a reflection that broadened my way of seeing and which in turn transformed my behaviour in my practice.

Maxine Greene (1991) describes the way in which literature can fuel such action as follows:

> And because it activates the imagination, it may well urge people to act, to transform, to repair in some fashion to their own inhabited space. This is especially so if a novel, instead of conforming to what readers know all too well, appeals to their indignation or, as Sartre puts it, discloses a social world animated by indignation
>
> (Greene, 1991, p. 258)

In order to be effective practitioners, Schön calls for the development of reflective practices, a balanced coming together of reflection and action. I suggest that literature and story can provide a means for fostering this praxis.

Our encounter with the literary world shapes our ways of seeing, our meanings, our consciousness and our selves, just as readily as our encounter with the 'real' world can shape these dimensions. In this way it can influence and inform the actions that we choose to make in the world. Therefore, 'the knowing made possible by literature may well be a moment of praxis' (Greene, 1991, p. 260) – a moment that informs the actions of health care practitioners in the 'real' world.

Limitations

One argument against using literature as a heuristic to learning in health professional education is that real and text worlds are typically characterised as a dichotomy between the two separate worlds of reality and fiction. Beach (1998) argues that this distinction between the 'real' as 'actual' and 'fiction' as make-believe is problematic, as our experience in 'real' contexts is shaped by our imaginative construction of alternative perspectives and roles. Likewise, our interpretations, and the meanings we discern from fiction, are shaped by real world contexts. Thus, literary fiction can provide an opportunity for a dialogue between the two worlds, so that a dialectic rather than a dichotomy is at play.

And yet it is important to note, as Maxine Greene (1991) does that:

> The reading of a demanding book can never guarantee the taking of transformative action. Practical judgements always have to be made in particular situations; connections have to be found between the interpretation – the seeing or the naming – and what Sartre and others speak of as praxis. (p. 261)

Thus, although literature and stories have the potential to transform, it is certainly not a given that growth or transformation will occur as a result of engagement with literary texts. In a sense it depends on the quality of the relationship between the subjectivity of the individual and the text at hand. The experiences that the reader brings to the text are also relevant to how it is taken up. It also depends on the relevance of the texts and how those texts are chosen, and this indeed is an important consideration beyond the scope of this chapter. In the end, as Bruner (1986) points out, 'it is the reader who must write for himself or herself what he or she intends to do with the actual text' (p. 24).

It is important to recognise, therefore, that although literature may offer benefits, it is not a panacea. Indeed, numerous factors interact with how a text is read and perceived. These include the quality and relevance of the text, who chooses the text and how it is chosen, the ensuing dialogue, and the subjectivity and life experience of the learner.

Conclusion

In summary, I suggest that literature can provide a heuristic – an approach for directing one's attention in learning – for health professional education, and is an educational approach that merits further consideration. As much work in the health professions is influenced by what occurs in the feeling structure, mind, imagination, and sensibility of living social beings, I draw attention above to how the literary arts can contribute to the education of health professionals in this regard. In this chapter I have discussed how engagement with literature can influence health practitioners to see in new ways, grasp new meanings, make changes in consciousness, transform their actions and develop praxis. Engagement with the literary arts has the potential to promote increased awareness and socially-responsive practice, within healthcare environments. While education in the health professions often focuses on scientific knowledge, the cultivation of attention to the lifeworld of the client, to the moral imagination of the practitioner – and to social, political, economic, discursive and cultural milieux in healthcare practice – has the potential to be heightened through engagement with the literary arts.

In closing, Maxine Greene's (1991) words depict the possibilities inherent in this approach: 'As with other arts, literature offers occasions to attend from the centre of a consciousness thrusting into the inter-subjective world' (p. 266). As living social beings this is a dimension that requires greater attention in the promotion of social change agendas in the education of health professionals. With respect to healthcare, Downie (1999) has proposed that we must seek competence and wisdom in our practitioners; competence from scientific training and wisdom from a broader notion of what it means to be educated. I am hopeful that in the future, rather than being characterised as subversive that literary and narrative approaches to health professional education will be characterised as necessary.

References

Beach, R. (1998) 'Constructing real and text worlds in responding to literature', *Theory into practice*, Vol. 37, No. 3, pp. 176–85.

Brookfield, S. (1987) *Developing critical thinkers*. Milton Keynes: Open University Press.

Bruner, J. (1986) *Actual minds, possible worlds*. Cambridge, MA: Harvard University Press.

Campo, R. (1997) *The poetry of healing*. New York, NY: Norton.

Carr, D. (1986) *Time, narrative, and history*. Bloomington, Indiana: Indiana University Press.

Coles, R. (1989) *The call of stories*. Boston, MA: Houghton Mifflin Company.

Darbyshire, P. (1995) 'Lessons from literature: Caring, interpretation, and dialogue', *Journal of Nurse Education*, Vol. 34, No. 5, pp. 211–16.

Downie, R. (1999) 'The role of literature in medical education', *Journal of Medical Ethics*, Vol. 25, No. 6, pp. 529–31.

Evans, M., Greaves, D. and Pickering, N. (1997) 'Medicine, the arts and imagination', *Journal of Medical Ethics*, Vol. 23, p. 254.

Frank, A. (1995) *The wounded storyteller: Body, illness and ethics*. Chicago, ILL: University of Chicago Press.

Freire, P. (1989) *Pedagogy of the oppressed*. New York: Continuum.

Garro, L. and Mattingly, C. (2000) 'Narrative as construct and construction'. In C. Mattingly and L. C. Garro (eds), *Narrative and the cultural construction of illness and healing* (pp. 1–49). Berkeley: University of California Press.

Gillon, R. (1997) 'Imagination, literature, medical ethics and medical practice', *Journal of Medical Ethics*, Vol. 23, pp. 3–4.

Gold, J. (1990) *Read for your life*. Markham, ON: Fitzhenry & Whiteside.

Greene, M. (1988) *The dialectic of freedom*. New York, NY: Teachers College Press.

Greene, M. (1991) 'Realizing literature's emancipatory potential'. In J. Mezirow and Associates, *Fostering critical reflection in adulthood: A guide to transformative and emancipatory learning* (pp. 251–68). San Francisco, CA: Jossey-Bass.

Greene, M. (1995) *Releasing the imagination: Essays on education, the arts, and social change*. San Francisco, CA; Jossey-Bass.

Iser, W. (1989) *Prospecting: From reader response to literary anthropology*. Baltimore: John Hopkins University Press.

Jarvis, C. (1999) 'Love changes everything: The transformative potential of popular romantic fiction', *Studies in the Education of Adults*, Vol. 31, No. 2, pp. 109–23.

Kinsella, E. A. (2005) 'Constructions of self: Ethical overtones in surprising locations', *Journal of Medical Ethics: Medical Humanities*, Vol. 31, No. 2, pp. 67–71.

Kinsella, E. A. (2006) 'Poetic resistance: Juxtaposing personal and professional discursive constructions in a practice context', *Journal of the Canadian Association for Curriculum Studies*, Vol. 4, No. 1, pp. 35–49.

Kleinman, A. (1988) *The illness narratives: Suffering, healing, and the human condition*. New York: Basic Books.

Kleinman, A. (1995) *Writing at the margin: Discourse between anthropology and medicine*. Berkeley and Los Angeles: University of California Press.

Lesser, W. (2002) *Nothing remains the same: Rereading and remembering*. Boston: Houghton Mifflin.

Lyotard, J. F. (1979) *The postmodern condition*. Manchester, UK: University of Manchester Press.

Marcuse, H. (1978) *The aesthetic dimension*. Boston: Beacon Press.

Mezirow, J. (1991) *Tranformative dimensions of adult learning*. San Francisco, CA: Jossey-Bass.

Mootoo, S. (1998) *Cereus blooms at night*. Toronto, ON: McClelland & Stewart.

Nelson, H. L. (2001) *Damaged identities: Narrative repair*. Ithaca, NY: Cornell University Press.

Nisker, J. (2001) 'Room for a view: Chalcedonies', *Canadian Medical Association Journal*, Vol. 164, No. 1, pp. 74–5.

Nisker, J. (2004) 'Narrative ethics in health care'. In J. Storch, P. Rodney and R. Starzomski (eds), *Toward a moral horizon: Nursing ethics for leadership and practice* (pp. 285–309). Toronto: Pearson-Prentice Hall.

Noddings, N. (1995) 'Care and moral education'. In W. Kohli (ed), *Critical conversations in philosophy of education*, pp. 137–48. New York: Routledge.

Nussbaum, M. (1990) *Love's knowledge: Essays on philosophy and literature*. New York: Oxford University Press.

Parsons, L. (2004) 'Challenging the gender divide: Improving literacy for all', *Teacher Librarian*, Vol. 32, No. 2, pp. 8–11.

Roach, M. S. (1998) 'Caring ontology: Ethics and the call of suffering', *International Journal of Human Caring*, Vol. 2, No. 2, pp. 30–4.

Sacks, O. (1985) *The man who mistook his wife for a hat*. New York, NY: Summit Books.

Schön, D. (1983) *The reflective practitioner*. New York: Basic Books.

Schön, D. (1987) *Educating the reflective practitioner*. San Francisco: Jossey-Bass.

Scott, P. (1997) 'Imagination in practice', *Journal of Medical Ethics*, Vol. 23, pp. 45–50.

Sewell, M. (ed) (1991) *Cries of the spirit.* Boston, MA: Beacon.

Simon, R. (1992) *Teaching against the grain: Texts for a pedagogy of possibility.* Toronto, ON: OISE Press.

Sumara, D. J. (1998) 'Fictionalizing acts: Reading and the making of identity', *Theory into practice,* Vol. 37, No. 3, pp. 203–10.

Sumara, D. J. (1996) *Private readings in public: Schooling the literary imagination.* New York: Peter Lang.

Tolstoy, L. (1954) *Anna Karenina.* Harmondsworth, UK: Penguin Books.

Townsend, E. (1998) *Good intentions overruled.* Toronto, ON: University of Toronto Press.

Van Manen, M. (2002) *Writing in the dark.* London, ON: Althouse Press.

Wendell, S. (1996) *The rejected body: Feminist philosophical reflections on disability.* New York: Routledge.

Winterson, J. (1995) *Art Objects.* New York, NY: Vintage Press.

Wright-St Clair, V. (2001) 'Caring: The moral motivation for good occupational therapy practice', *Australian Occupational Therapy Journal,* Vol. 48, pp. 187–99.

Section Two

The emancipatory potential
of arts-based adult education

CHAPTER 3

Everyone performs, everyone has a place

Camp fYrefly and arts-informed, community-based education, cultural work and inquiry

André P. Grace and Kristopher Wells

Introduction

In this chapter we explore Camp fYrefly, a summer camp we created to help build and nurture leadership potential in lesbian, gay, bisexual, trans-identified, two-spirited, queer, and allied (LGBTTQ&A) youths between the ages of 14 and 24. This annual camp provides a contemporary example of arts-informed, community-based education, cultural work and inquiry. It takes place in Edmonton, Alberta, Canada, and it aims to help LGBTTQ&A youths learn how to make significant contributions to their own lives and to their schools, home/group-home environments, and communities. To capture the tenor and energy of Camp fYrefly, the chapter begins with André's poetic reflection of what transpired during the third annual summer camp in July 2006. This leads into an overview of the camp, surveying its philosophy, dynamics, and purposes. We follow this conspectus with a discussion about queer bodies and queer theory as we consider youth participants and their positionalities in relation to mediating the camp environment and the larger culture and society. Then we engage in multi-perspective theorising that juxtaposes critical ethnography and postmodern aesthetics with arts-based inquiry to frame our cultural education and leadership work at the camp. We share some of the participants' written reflections on Camp fYrefly. We conclude with a perspective about how we situate the camp as an arts↔expressive space.

Camp fYrefly's synergy comes from the efforts of a collective of educators, artists, dramatists, musicians, writers, and other cultural workers. They volunteer their time and strive to provide a space where youths and young adults can become resilient as they resist and reject heterosexism, homophobia, and transphobia, and envision and enact a healthy and happy future free from fear, abuse, discrimination, and righteous stereotyping. By developing a human-and-material resource network of LGBTTQ&A friends, trusted adults, community resources, and leadership strategies, we hope that youths will be able to thrive and become transformative leaders who advocate for social justice and inclusion in their schools, families (as they construct them), and local communities. This goal is at the heart of social education and learning in informal and non-formal settings (Grace & Hill, 2004; Grace, Hill, Johnson & Lewis, 2004).

Queer Body Magic

They pile in
With knapsacks and hopes
With CD players and fears
Some who came to Camp fYrefly before shout out
As they recognise the faces of returning queer friends
Eyes light up
Recognition is good
Some stand tall
Hugs happen
Queer body magic

There are no types
There are no stereotypes
Just a room full of queers
Les-bi-gay-trans-two-spirit-straight-and-other queers

Queers everywhere
No binaries are allowed here
You don't have to be confined to either/or choices
Like a homo or a hetero
Or a girl or a boy
You just have to be you capturing the sweetness of queer youth

The trauma of the outside world seems forgotten as youths mingle
It surfaces though in the reminders of struggling young bodies
Reminders like too much medication
Too many special diets
Too many anxious faces
Some youths need to cry
Everyone needs to talk
As newcomers settle into the safe but unfamiliar queer space
They muster the trust and courage to say 'hi' to newfound queer kin
We love the din of voices found, of voices carried

Peers seasoned by previous queer camp experiences lead the way
Rallying newcomers to find a medium
A way to express themselves
It starts with making your own mailbox from a lantern-shaped takeout
    container
Each youth creates something personal, something special
Leaving an imprint that uses words and symbols
To name and represent a unique queer who came to queer camp
Suddenly each box looks different
And ready to be stuffed with 'happy notes'
Encouraging words that everyone will write one another during the
    camp

The camp shifts into gear
A role-play allows you to be someone else if you're not quite ready to
    be yourself
Apprehensive bodies begin to relax
The catharsis of arts-informed activities let's you breathe again
The camp has a circadian rhythm that draws energy from the artistic
    expression

And still each day becomes more eclectic, more electric
The desire to share and perform heightens
It's knowing me, knowing you, and informing others
The peaks are the nightly talent shows
We are what we are and what we express

A boy lets the girl inside come out
She's a wonderful singer
A girl lets the boy inside come out
A rap star is born
Everyone performs
Everyone has a place
There are poets and storytellers
Songwriters and singers
Dancers and jugglers
Illusionists and acrobats

This is it
Queers being
Queers becoming and queers belonging
Living the performance
Enjoying the moment
Capturing it in this time and space with queer kin
There are no empty spots on the program
Just encores and joyful noise
And more hugs
Queer body magic

André P. Grace

About Camp f Yrefly

André's introductory poem captures aspects of the socio-cultural milieu that has emerged at Camp f Yrefly. As mentioned above, the camp is a personal, social, and cultural learning retreat for LGBTTQ&A youths. It focuses on building and nurturing their leadership potential in an effort to help them learn how to make more active contributions to their schools, home/group-home environments, and communities. Camp fYrefly recognises the diversity of the LGBTTQ&A youths who participate. When they register for the camp, we ask the youth to tell us about any previous leadership experiences they may have had in volunteer or other situations. At camp, we emphasise take and give: take what you need from the camp and give back to other youths through subsequent community involvement. This year 55 youths attended the camp, and we hope to be able to expand our capacity in the future.

To our knowledge, Camp fYrefly is the only LGBTTQ&A youth-leadership camp of its kind in Canada. Camp programming uses a by-youth-for-youth approach in which older youths (really young adults) who have already had leadership training in previous camps or through our Out Is In project (Grace & Wells, 2007) mentor younger youths.

In the spirit of advancing youth leadership, a youth advisory panel guides the development and delivery of a wide-ranging leadership-and-learning programme. A support team of adult mentor-volunteers assists; it includes adult educators, schoolteachers, artists, musicians, dramatists, dancers, writers, police officers, psychologists, clergy and queer cultural workers. Collectively, everyone helps to create workshops and activities that emphasise self-development, healthy socialisation and social learning, empowerment, critical reflection, consciousness-raising, and anti-oppression work. Youths chose the name Camp fYrefly, constructing the acronym to stand for fostering, Youth, resiliency, energy, fun, leadership, yeah! This description captures what Camp fYrefly is all about.

Planning for the next annual Camp fYrefly starts in early autumn after everyone has had time to rejuvenate and process what went on at the previous camp. The camp features day and evening activities and workshops focused on an array of topics that include facilitation and presentation skill-building, confronting bias and dealing with diversity, coming to terms with sex, sexual and gender differences, negotiating relationships with parents and caregivers, and promoting youth health and safety. At the heart of the camp is the idea of fighting oppression through the arts and participatory drama and other arts-based activities as social learning to help youths network, build self-esteem and nurture their own knowledge about society and self.

The camp also involves guest speakers who, over three camps, have included a two-spirited Elder, an out lesbian police officer, a gay politician in Edmonton's municipal government, Edmonton's gay-activist Police Commissioner, a bisexual songwriter, an affirming United Church minister, a gay journalist, a trans-identified teacher, a lesbian psychologist, a trans-identified pastor, and a gay social worker. Providing opportunities for youths to dialogue with queer role models has been a salient element of the camp. As well, camp planners build in designated time for personal reflection, community building, games, and social activities.

Who comes to camp? Talking about queer bodies

LGBTTQ&A youths talk about their bodies and their embodied and embedded selves. They know that queer bodies have histories as typed, stereotyped, aberrant, and pathologised objects in a heterosexualising culture, histories that get in the way of queer being, becoming, and belonging. They also know that they are part of a queer spectrum of persons with sex, sexual, and gender differences. They learn that this spectrum often feigns community, but it is not one. Queer history teaches them that some gays have left out lesbians, some lesbians have left out male-to-female transsexuals, some white queers have left out queers of colour, and so on. This amounts to a domino effect that reproduces exclusion as a marker of queer as well as the dominant culture. LGBTTQ&A youths focused on inclusion and cultural transformation reject this history, which they associate with typing, stereotyping, and fixedness. As they try to make sense of their queer bodies, they associate them with shifting identities and fluid positionalities. Boys don't have to be boys as conceived in heterosexualising language and perception. And girls don't have to be girls. Gender identity and sexual orientation do not have to be fixed for life.

All of this complicates desire and its expression, and it means rethinking normalcy and acceptability in everyday behaviour. For example, in a contestation of the boundedness of gendered physical spaces, youth participants at Camp fYrefly decided that there would be no male or female washrooms, simply un-gendered washrooms. As youths developed rules and a protocol based on an ethic of mutual respect for all youths present, they felt that this declassification of washrooms was important. Of course, many youths were still concerned with privacy and personal comfort, especially when it came to showering.

Youths problem-solved by installing more privacy curtains in the shower area, and by creating a sign-up sheet to accommodate those who wanted individual showering times.

As academics in another part of our lives, this problem-solving around the rejection of binary classification provides a lived example of engaging queer theory in the everyday. We are reminded here of Fuss's (1991) theorising in her essay entitled *Inside/out*, which constituted a pivotal moment in the emergence of queer theory. In her theorising, Fuss called for wide-awake, unwavering work from/on the margins and for a border-crossing theory to address the pervasiveness and fluidity of sex, sexual, and gender differences. She suggested that this work begin by challenging the legitimated cultural status of heterosexuality as a compulsory identity, practice, and institution that contests what it perceives as 'the continual predatory encroachments of its contaminated other, homosexuality' (p. 2). For Fuss, this means understanding that traditional binaries like heterosexual/homosexual and male/female are socially, culturally, and historically based on an inside/out binary that locates queer doing and desiring on the outside 'based on a logic of limits, margins, borders and boundaries' (p. 1).

It is obvious to us that Generation Q rejects this logic (Grace & Wells, 2001, 2005). As LGBTTQ&A youths see it, such constricting logic places limits on sexual positionality and desire. This is achieved 'variously and in tandem, through acts and experiences of defense, ambivalence, repression, denial, threat, trauma, injury, identification, internalization, and renunciation' (Fuss, 1991, p. 2). The result is the alienation of the many queers who exist in the spectral spaces found between the heterosexual/homosexual and male/female binary ends. As they contest the containment that binaries trigger, LGBTTQ&A youths seek increased presence and visibility. However, we caution youths here in the interest of their safety because enhanced cultural exposure can intensify homophobia and transphobia, resulting in increased reprisal and backlash.

It is increasingly clear to us that today's LGBTTQ&A youths are different. Savin-Williams (2005) speaks to this transition in his book *The new gay teenager*. While the idea of queer youths as 'at-risk' and the earlier idea of queer youths as deviant, pathological, and in need of specialised medical intervention still have currency in some (usually conservative politico-religious) circles, Savin-Williams tells us that queer youths are now being characterised in new, more respectful, and affirming ways. He relates that educational and cultural interventions used since the late 1990s emphasise youth resilience or developmental assets. These interventions have also focused on the creation of safe spaces and anti-harassment policy development as more queer youths engage in advocacy and civil-rights work.

In Canada, queer youths have been emboldened by rapid and significant gains made in legal and legislative arenas. They know they have equality rights and privileges as queer Canadians (Grace, 2005; Grace & Wells, 2005). Savin-Williams suggests this kind of sociocultural change may nurture a new characterisation of queer youths as they adopt a 'post-gay' positionality where sexuality is no longer considered the defining aspect of their personhood. As Savin-Williams argues, the everyday ordinariness of the spectrum of sex, sexual, and gender differences may well become the defining feature of LGBTTQ&A youths. Anonymous Queers (1999) consider this an expansion of the space of sex, sexual, and gender geography.

> Being queer is not about a right to privacy; it is about the freedom to be public, to just be who we are. It means everyday fighting oppression, homophobia, racism, misogyny, the bigotry of religious hypocrites and our own self-hatred . . . It's about being on the margins, defining ourselves; it's about gender-fuck and secrets, what's beneath the belt and deep inside the heart; it's about the night. (p. 588)

Of course, as increasing numbers of today's LGBTTQ&A youths see it, it is also about naming, shouting out loud, resisting, and NOT being anonymous.

Engendering a jolt to the unconscious: Multi-perspective theorising and inquiry in our educational and cultural work

Living out and studying queer lives are complicated, contentious, political, and value-laden endeavours that take place in the culture-language-power nexus where matters of context, disposition, and relationship play out. In working with LGBTTQ&A youths, and attending to the power relationship between the researcher and the researched, we have relied on multi-perspective theorising to help us find our way in a lived process of arts-informed, community-based education, cultural work, and inquiry. This process demands that we act ethically and be responsive and responsible, performative and watchful. As educators, mentors, and researchers, we feel we are always involved in a kind of social evolution in which we are always coming to know the changing queer youth in our care.

Our work takes place in the intersection of the moral and the political. A turn to critical ethnography helps us here. As a way to research people and their lived and learned experiences in the complex intersection of culture, language, power, and social locations, critical ethnography requires us to engage issues of ethical practice, social and cultural democracy, queer individual and collective freedom, and justice. As a research method and a culture-power practice, critical ethnography challenges us to speak from a historically- and culturally-located standpoint as we build local queer working knowledge and interrogate the heterosexual/homosexual and male/female binaries that position us all – the researchers and the researched. In speaking to this function of critical ethnography, Foley and Valenzuela (2005) ask us to confront our locatedness as 'mere culture-bound mortals' (p. 218). Moreover, they ask us to remember the specificity of our educational and cultural work and research: 'Because all standpoints represent particular interests and positions in a hierarchical society, they are "ideological" in the sense that they are partial' (p. 218). The upshot of focusing on locatedness, as Foley and Valenzuela see it, is that both the researchers and the researched can pay special attention to subjective ways of knowing and the intuitive in the arts-informed work and research that we do. This helps youths as research participants to build self-knowledge and to understand how it emerges in historical and cultural contexts and in relation to others in their circle of interaction. In this regard, youths learn that being, becoming, and belonging are political processes always touched by matters of context, disposition, and relationship.

Engaging Camp fYrefly as a participatory educational, cultural, and critical research project is never easy. Methodologically, we take up the politics and dynamics of researching the researcher and engaging research participants as we use archetypal ethnographic and other qualitative methods. These include participant observation, open-ended interviews, focus groups, arts-informed inquiry, and narrative inquiry via poetry and narrative vignettes. Here it is vital to focus on issues of rapport, trust, dialogic connectedness, and the involvement of the researchers and the researched in an iterative process of making sense and meaning of research knowledge.

From an ethical perspective, we have to be clear why we would integrate research into our educational and cultural work with LGBTTQ&A youths. As we see it, the research has to be with them, about them, and for them. Foley and Valenzuela relate that critical ethnography can help in raising consciousness. This is a key focus for us. We hope our research with youths provides them with yet another opportunity to build queer self-knowledge and sociocultural knowledge. We also hope that youths will use this knowledge to raise public consciousness of being, becoming, and belonging as queer persons and citizens. For example, for those LGBTTQ&A youths who feel comfortable and able, we organise opportunities for them to be interviewed so their words and artistic creations find their way into newspapers, magazines, and television segments. On the one hand, we want to teach youths to be media-savvy, and to help them to identify and address the risks that come with media exposure. On the other hand, we want youths to have voice and visibility as they work to make a better world for themselves and their queer kin.

As part of multi-perspective theorising in our educational and cultural work and inquiry, we juxtapose our work in critical ethnography with work in postmodern aesthetics. This lets us focus on notions like positionality and fluid identity, which are absent in critical discourse. We do this because 'ethnography must always be a provisional space' (St. Pierre, 1997, p. 379). Juxtaposing what may be competing theories helps to create tensions in our work that help us see what is problematic about critical and postmodern perspectives and any border crossing between them.

Slattery (2006) helps us in understanding and engaging postmodern aesthetics. In his postmodern approach to curriculum development, he places the arts at the centre of pedagogy, classroom practice, and individual growth and development. Slattery views arts-based research as a way to show how art forms can be used as a curricular device 'to advance justice, compassion, and postmodern sensibilities' (p. 258). He explains, 'Film, poetry, visual images, music, dance, drama, and literature are vehicles for engendering the jolt to the unconscious that leads to the autobiographical narrative, which is essential if mere schooling is to become educative and transformative' (p. 260). At a time when instrumentality appears to have primary value in curriculum development, Slattery considers it urgent to give renewed priority to art forms in the teaching–learning interaction. He declares, '[P]ostmodern education encourages aesthetic reflections from the heart in educational inquiry' (p. 243). Slattery wants us to see and relate to people as perceptive subjects with imagination and intuition: 'Experiential, autobiographical, and metaphorical reflection' (p. 244) help in achieving this subjectivity. Engaging in such reflection, one youth created a drawing that sequenced the stages in coming out and coming to terms as personally conceived. The ball represents queer as a secret that is hidden at first, then shared, and ultimately celebrated.

We must be careful, though, as we engage a diverse LGBTTQ&A youth population in this kind of reflection that goes to the heart and soul of who an individual is. For example, queer youths may equate such reflection with revisiting trauma or re-enacting turmoil. Many of them have lived with hurt, silence, indignity, invisibility, tears, fear, frustration, anger, weakness, and sometimes just enough resilience to manage to

'The Secret' – Using art and autobiography to explore the Self and Other

survive. Self-destructive behaviours and suicide ideation or attempts are pervasive phenomena among queer youths (Friend, 1998; Ryan & Futterman, 1998; Wells, 2006). While self-exploration using art forms can contribute to building self-knowledge, self-esteem, and resilience, an ethic of caring for and protecting queer youths must always guide educational and cultural work and inquiry with them. As responsive and responsible educators and researchers, we must be present, involved, and discerning as we engage LGBTTQ&A youths in an arts-based discovery of self and others that amounts to 'border crossing, a seminal moment, a synthetical event' (Slattery, 2006, p. 246).

As we bring history and politics to bear on understanding experi-ence in arts-based inquiry, Walsh (2006) reminds us that we mediate a 'process through which we can come to (re)write and . . . (re)read experience, to open possibilities, to feel, and to (re)member something different' (p. 978). She considers this an 'attempt to dis-cover how we have been shaped to read our experiences in particular ways and why we have agreed to such readings' (pp. 978–9). To make sense of experience, Finley (2005), in her version of the genealogy of arts-based inquiry, suggests that we start from the common social-science belief that inquiry 'is always moral and political' (p. 681). In interpreting this belief, she asserts that those who hold it should be 'purposeful in performing inquiry that is activist, engages in public criticism, and is resistant to neoconservative discourses that threaten social justice' (p. 681). Thus located, performativity helps constitute a dynamic equilibrium between research and practice. Of course, the performers in this work are not just those educated in the arts. Indeed, Finley (2005) asserts that a focus on pure art and quality control assaults exploratory postmodern aesthetics that are inclusive.

> Performativity is the quality criterion . . . necessary to achieve arts-based approaches to inquiry that . . . purposefully intends to facilitate critical race, indigenous, queer, and feminist and border studies as entrée to multiple, new, and diverse ways of understanding and living in the world. (p. 693)

In an example of performativity as an educational and cultural practice, youth participants in a camp workshop entitled *Using popular theatre to create change* learned how to use drama techniques as tools to share opinions and facilitate dialogue about oppression in relation to queer being, becoming, and belonging. The workshop helped youths to use their own experiences to create simple, interactive role-plays, tableaux, and other drama activities. No acting expertise was necessary. Youths built knowledge about participation, expression, networking, and communicative action. In another sense-making session, youth participants performed by creating a graffiti wall as an information mural that described aspects of the queer self and self–social interaction. Here we asked them to take up a question: 'What does it mean to be a sexual-minority youth?' In answering, one group created the following panel for the graffiti wall that spoke to 'being me' in personal and relational terms.

To help them focus, the youths, following Bennett and Rolheiser-Bennett (2001), constructed the graffiti wall using a PMI (plus, minus, interesting) thinking organiser. Creating the graffiti wall became a way for participants to engage in a creative mind-mapping process that involved collecting the ideas and wisdom of everyone in the group. As the youths worked individually and collectively, they expressed themselves using words and symbols. The finished graffiti wall became an art installation to which others at the camp could contribute during

A 'Being Me' graffiti wall panel at Camp fYrefly

free time. The art installation became a central element in the local CFRN Canadian Television Network's coverage of the camp (Mah, 2005), enabling the graffiti wall to be a vehicle for public consciousness-raising. The youths were able to share the content and meaning of the graffiti wall with a larger audience as an example of public pedagogy that reveals and demystifies. A DVD of this CFRN/CTV coverage enables a continued sharing of the graffiti-wall messages with new audiences, extending the public pedagogical moment (Mah, 2005). This is in keeping with Finley's (2005) view that '[m]aking art is a passionate visceral activity that creates opportunities for communion among participants, researchers, and the various audiences who encounter the [art form as a communicative and] research text' (p. 685). This cultural work captures 'the artfulness to be found in everyday living,' and it aims 'to bring about culturally situated, political aesthetics that are responsive to social dilemmas' (p. 686). These aesthetics, Finley suggests, incorporate the imaginative, the communal, the experiential, the perceptual, the emotional, and the sensual.

> [They] create spaces for dialogues that blur boundaries among researchers, participants, and audiences so that, ideally, roles reverse and participants lead researchers to new questions, audiences revert to questioning practitioners, and so forth as all interact within one text. In this instance, the text is defined in the broadest possible terms and invokes all of the actions in the world that can be 'read.' (p. 686)

From a research perspective, studying LGBTTQ&A youths, their artistic creations, and the interactive moments they engender amounts to participating in a kind of proactive, critical postmodern, action-based inquiry that emphasises positionality, expression, and communication within a research practice that highlights ethics, justice, and individual and cultural freedom. Here, the researchers and the researched work together to record, communicate, interpret, and deliberate in order to further processes of consciousness-raising and cultural change. Such research as border crossing has the potential to be 'expressive research that portrays the multidimensionality of [queer] human life' (Finley, 2005, p. 683). Finley maintains that expressive research as performativity is fortified by art forms, politics, and pedagogy.

For us, art forms have been tools for communication and engagement in our educational and cultural work and in our arts-informed educational research. Eisner (2006) is an inspiration here. Artistry is performativity in his eyes.

> Artistry is the ability to craft a performance, influence its pace, shape its rhythms and tone so its parts merge into a coherent whole. Artistry in teaching depends on embodied knowledge. The body plays a central role; it tunes you in to what's going on. You come to feel a process that often exceeds the capacity of language to describe. (p. 45)

Eisner (2005) links this notion of a whole performance to the notion of a whole student. He asks us to remember Dewey's progressive call to engage the whole student who responds intellectually, imaginatively, emotionally, and socially in the teaching–learning interaction. From this perspective, it is important that our interactions with LGBTTQ&A youths at Camp fYrefly are organic, acknowledging and accommodating camp participants as historical and cultural human subjects caught up in the social and the political. Eisner calls this engagement 'cultivating productive idiosyncrasy' (p. 16), which is nurturing the particular and the situated. To achieve this goal, he calls on us 'to support the pursuit of cognitive surprise, the creation of intrinsic forms of motivation, the development of imagination, . . . [and] the ability to define and resolve one's problems' (p. 17). As Eisner sees it, engaging in the arts enables us to reach these ends in order to develop the whole student through a merger of cognition with emotion.

In the intersection of the affective and the affirmative: LGBTTQ&A youths speak out

LGBTTQ&A youths constitute the energy and *raison d'être* for Camp fYrefly. At the end of each camp, we ask youth participants to respond to a survey based on their camp experiences of being, becoming, and belonging. The responses to the survey are analysed by youth leaders and adult facilitators as a starting point in the process of planning the next annual camp. This is part of our by-youth-for youth approach that enables youth leaders to link youth voices from the survey to action in terms of remembering what things are important to youths as we make improvements for the next camp. We provide this collage of their comments and reflections.

> Right off the bat we weren't strangers – just a group that was gathering for the first time.

> I came and no one judged me or made opinions about me without getting to know me.

> There were so many of us. Everyone was so happy, friendly, and energetic.
> Everyone was treated with so much respect.

> We talked openly about never having felt so supported and safe, and we realised that some youths do not have family and/or a support network.

> The whole experience was so emotional. In fact, the abundance of emotion that was displayed was really unexpected and quite touching.

> I was so content and comfortable. I guess it was because I was surrounded by those who just knew.

> The emotional drama exercise taught me about my own insecurities.

> I didn't have to be afraid. I could say 'my girlfriend' and nobody blinked an eye.

> Our short stories and poems triggered compassion and support from others regardless of age.

> We had a hug fest.

Collectively, these comments provide testament to the importance of the affective and the affirmative at our summer camp. Indeed camaraderie, mutual respect, and open communication are the hallmarks of Camp fYrefly. However, what is truly most intriguing is the speed at which these dynamics become an omnipresent and natural part of camp culture. We credit this to the arts-informed educational and cultural work that drives the camp. The opportunities to write and share poetry and narrative vignettes, to engage in improvised theatre, to create a graffiti wall, to craft a cartoon, and to dance expressively so that movement removes the need for words become some of the ways that the arts live in, inspire, and energise youths during Camp fYrefly. Perhaps this expression is most profoundly conveyed during the nightly talent shows, as André's poem indicates. Artistic expression enables you to be who you really are. And if you are not ready yet, it enables you to portray who you would really like to be once you deal with all the queer baggage.

We now provide two examples to indicate how the youths used art in the intersection of the affective and the affirmative at Camp fYrefly. Kaitlin, age 20, has attended all three summer camps. She is one of our youth leaders. Kaitlin is working on a 'zine so camp participants can continue to share their writing, cartoons, and other creations with one another throughout the year. She wrote this narrative vignette to reflect on her camp experience.

In the Glow

I went to a Camp called Camp fYrefly (because each of us has a light inside) and I felt wonderful and calm and happy, and I couldn't figure it out.

There were workshops happening and people getting emotional, and I thought, 'Why am I not feeling it?' Then it dawned on me, and as we sat in a circle in a field, I shared my epiphany with everyone. I told them how I was feeling so content and how I couldn't really figure it out, and then I realised . . . I felt safe, happy, and comfortable because they were all not straight on some level. We were all just so comfortable and I realised that I could just be myself in every way. I could be a Drag King in the talent show.

I am always mostly myself . . . but I have to admit that because of my sexual orientation, I often feel something lacking. Something that is comfortable and safe that's just not there . . . It's in the inability for me to share my love for a movie that just happens to have two girls in love as the main characters, or the inability to share with my parents a relationship that goes beyond friendship, or the inability to speak about how a girl made my heart flutter without having someone avert their eyes or stop the conversation. It's no one's fault really . . . they just don't relate. But this weekend everyone could relate and I was so completely happy because, for the first time in my entire life, I was completely whole in every way. It wasn't about talking about how we were all gay. It was about being pure, whole, safe, and together as a kind of community.

I wish we could all love everything about each other: everything that makes us similar and, especially, everything that sets us apart – makes us the individuals we are. I wish we could all be comfortable with the different experiences that every person has and that we could all realise that there is only one race . . . the human race . . . and we're all in it together. I'm happy because I found something I think I had lost after leaving my local youth group. For a little while each week that gay and lesbian youth group gave me a feeling of unity. I have met some amazing, astounding, and marvelous people during the camp, and I know that there are friendships being built that will last forever.

All I can do is smile because I realise that while my sexual orientation is not all of who I am . . . it's still a part of me, and it cannot be ignored or seen as less important for the sake of making those around me feel more comfortable.

I like girls . . . occasionally boys, but girls over all and over everything. I like to read, and I am obsessed with writing. I'm anxious and paranoid on occasion. I love dancing like no one's watching and singing at a karaoke bar. I have rainbow-colored hair because rainbows are for equality, and I believe in the equality of opportunity for every person, every living being. I believe we should all have the chance to live our lives, as we would love to, and that no one should ever hold us back from letting the light inside shine out.

Patrick came to camp for the first time in 2005 at age 14. He had just come out to his parents who never stopped loving and supporting him – this unconditional acceptance is crucial. His mom contacted us to ask questions about Camp fYrefly. We have seen Patrick mature and blossom this past year. He is building the skills to become one of our youth leaders. Patrick wrote this poem, which he shared one evening during a talent show.

The Newest Glow

When I was alive
They called me Puppet
And all my friends did
Was pull my strings

When I had a boyfriend
He called me muffin when he kissed me sweetly
But all my friends did
Was cut my strings

When I had friends
We laughed together
But then I realised
They were laughing at me

When I was alone
I found only one love burning bright at my side
And it came in the shape
Of a warm, glowing fYrefly

Concluding perspective:
Articulating Camp fYrefly as an arts↔expressive space

In this chapter we have worked in the intersection of theoretical and practical articulations of arts-informed, community-based education, cultural work, and inquiry. We realise that this place can be a challenging, even disconcerting space for some. However, it is a very comfortable space for us. Critical postmodern theorising has given us a place and a way to deal with practice and its tensions when diverse spaces in real life and many people have not. Thus our education and cultural work moves with theory and through it. We keep theory at the heart of what we do, working from Giroux's premise that theory is 'a borderland where conversations begin, differences confront each other, hopes are initiated, and social struggles are waged' (cited in Tierney, 1993, p. x). From this critical postmodern perspective, we have gauged Camp fYrefly as a cultural practice and an ethical research space that has highlighted the positionalities of youths and their freedom to be learners, artists, and citizens in holistic and expressive ways. This is education, cultural work, and inquiry for social justice and transformation. It situates Camp fYrefly as a democratic engagement that emphasises notions of resistance and resiliency and encourages youths to be, become, and belong in the fullness of their sexual orientations and gender identities.

This focus on an individual's positionality at Camp fYrefly is coupled with an emphasis on social and cultural learning through the arts. We present the arts as multiple media that engage youths in processes of expression, reception, engagement, interpretation, and communication. We maintain that the focus of arts-informed education and cultural work is to accept and accommodate youths, to enable and sustain them. In this light, the arts as multiple media become bridges leading to accommodation and sustenance as youths move from silence and invisibility to expression that is solicited, safe, welcomed, nurtured, and valued. In this light, arts-informed educational and cultural work help Camp fYrefly to achieve its primary goal: to help sexual-minority youths to move from hiding and feeling ashamed about their differences to owning them, feeling them, embracing them, and living them.

Authors' Note: For more information about Camp fYrefly, please visit our website at www.fyrefly.ualberta.ca.

References

Anonymous Queers. (1999) 'Queers read this: I hate straights', In L. Gross and J. D. Woods (eds), *The Columbia reader on lesbians and gay men in media, society, and politics* (pp. 588–94). New York: Columbia University Press.

Bennett, B. B. and Rolheiser-Bennett, N. C. (2001) *Beyond Monet: The artful science of instructional integration*. Toronto: Bookation.

Eisner, E. (2005) 'Back to whole', *Educational Leadership*, Vol. 63, No. 1, pp. 14–18.

Eisner, E. (2006) 'The satisfactions of teaching', *Educational Leadership*, Vol. 63, No. 6, pp. 44–6.

Finley, S. (2005) 'Arts-based inquiry: Performing revolutionary pedagogy'. In N. K. Denzin and Y. S. Lincoln (eds), *The Sage handbook of qualitative research* (3rd ed.) (pp. 681–94). Thousand Oaks, CA: Sage Publications.

Foley, D. and Valenzuela, A. (2005) 'Critical ethnography: The politics of collaboration.' In N. K. Denzin and Y. S. Lincoln (eds), *The Sage handbook of qualitative research* (3rd ed.) (pp. 217–34). Thousand Oaks, CA: Sage Publications.

Friend, R. A. (1998) 'Heterosexism, homophobia, and the culture of schooling'. In S. Books (ed), *Invisible children in the society and its schools* (pp. 137–66). Mahwah, NJ: Lawrence Erlbaum Associates.

Fuss, D. (1991) 'Inside/out'. In D. Fuss (ed), *Inside/out: Lesbian theories, gay theories* (pp. 1–10). New York: Routledge.

Grace, A. P. (2005) 'Lesbian, gay, bisexual, and trans-identified (LGBT) teachers and students and the post-Charter quest for ethical and just treatment in Canadian schools'. A paper presented as a featured pre-sentation to the Canadian Teachers' Federation at the *Building Inclusive Schools: A Search for Solutions* Conference, Ottawa Marriott Hotel, Ottawa, ON. Retrieved September 23, 2006, from http://www. teachers.ab.ca/Issues+In+Education/Diversity+and+Human+Rights/ Sexual+Orientation/Publications/index.htm

Grace, A. P. and Hill, R. J. (2004) 'Positioning Queer in adult education: Intervening in politics and praxis in North America', *Studies in the Education of Adults*, Vol. 36, No. 2, pp. 167–89.

Grace, A. P., Hill, R. J., Johnson, C. W. and Lewis, J. B. (2004) 'In other words: Queer voices/dissident subjectivities impelling social change', *International Journal of Qualitative Studies in Education*, Vol. 17, No. 3, pp. 301–23.

Grace, A. P. and Wells, K. (2001) 'Getting an education in Edmonton, Alberta: The case of queer youth', *Torquere, Journal of the Canadian Lesbian and Gay Studies Association*, Vol. 3, pp. 137–51.

Grace, A. P. and Wells, K. (2005) 'The Marc Hall prom predicament: Queer individual rights v. institutional church rights in Canadian public education', *Canadian Journal of Education*, Vol. 28, No. 3, pp. 237–70.

Grace, A. P. and Wells, K. (2007) 'Using Freirean pedagogy of just ire to inform critical social learning in arts-informed community education for sexual minorities', *Adult Education Quarterly*, Vol. 57, No. 2, pp. 95–114.

Mah, S. (2005) *Camp fYrefly* [Television broadcast, DVD format]. Edmonton, AB: CFRN/CTV.

Ryan, C. and Futterman, D. (1998) *Lesbian and gay youth: Care & counseling*. New York: Columbia University Press.

Savin-Williams, R. C. (2005) *The new gay teenager*. Cambridge, MA: Harvard University Press.

Slattery, P. (2006) *Curriculum development in the postmodern era* (2nd ed.). New York: Routledge.

St. Pierre, E. (1997) 'Nomadic inquiry in the smooth spaces of the field: A preface', *International Journal of Qualitative Studies in Education*, Vol. 10, No. 3, pp. 365–83.

Tierney, W. G. (1993) *Building communities of difference*, Toronto: OISE Press.

Walsh, S. (2006) 'An Irigarayan framework and resymbolization in an arts-informed research process', *International Journal of Qualitative Studies in Education*, Vol. 12, No. 5, pp. 976–93.

Wells, K. (2006) *The gay–straight student alliance handbook: A comprehensive resource for K-12 teachers, administrators, and school counsellors*. Ottawa, ON: The Canadian Teachers' Federation.

CHAPTER 4

Tapestries through the making

Quilting as a valuable medium of feminist adult education and arts-based inquiry

Darlene E. Clover

The backing

For decades feminist adult educators have used arts and crafts to help women learn to break silences, become economically independent and explore social issues. Similarly, growing numbers of feminist researchers are moving towards creative, arts-based methods of research to explore issues affecting women's lives (Ball, 2002; Butterwick, 2002; Clover & Stalker, 2005). Yet it can be argued that the contributions these aesthetic activities make to feminist adult education and research are still not fully understood nor explored (Clover, Stalker & McGauley, 2004; Jongeward, 1994).

As a feminist adult educator who recently began to use the arts as/in my research, developing a deeper understanding of the contribution aesthetics can make is very important to me. In this chapter I explore how a creative, multilayered, and multidimensional quilting project titled *Sexual exploitation has no borders* adds to discourses of feminist adult education and arts-based inquiry. My reflections and analyses of this project are also informed by other explorations I have made into women, arts, and adult education over the past four years.

In deference to fabric creation, I tell the story of this project using the metaphoric language of the quilting world. The process of quilting proceeds in four distinct stages. First the backing is assembled and that is this section. This is followed by the construction of the foundational pieces – key conceptual framings and debates in feminist adult education and arts-based inquiry. A template is used for my description and thoughts on the four-phase learning, research, and dissemination process as well as the storied images stitched or painted into the fabric. Finally the appliqué detail is added; discussions of aspects I feel make a dynamic and valuable contribution to feminist adult education and arts-based inquiry.

The foundation piecing

Feminist adult education arose as a challenge to a field which had all but excluded the experiences, concerns and needs of women (Thompson, 1997). Of particular importance were issues such as rape, domestic violence, prostitution, and inequalities in terms of employment and education opportunities. Although feminist adult educators have broadened this list to include issues such as the environment and global-isation which greatly affect women (e.g. Clover, Stalker & McGauley, 2004; Walters, 1997), sexual violence and abuse remain key concerns (e.g. Horsman, 2000).

Drawing on discourses of social activism and learning for a just and equitable re-organisation of society, feminist adult education works towards the 'substantive transformation of women's lives and conditions' (Walters & Manicom, 1996, p. 3). Fundamental to this transformation is the active participation of women in their own learning and empower-ment in terms of the sexist and oppressive practices and ideologies ingrained in the fabric of society.

Walters and Manicom (1996) note that deeply embedded, yet highly contested, within feminist adult education discourse is the 'practical/ strategic couplet' (p. 13). On the one hand, it is argued that we need to focus on women's daily lived experiences, the practical and often more personal needs of women as these are the most immediate and known (Doerge, 1992). Others, however, suggest that it is strategic interests or political concerns that require the most attention because unless the personal or localised 'process is informed by an appreciation and analysis of the broader developments that are refracted in the local mileux, constraining and shaping local possibilities, its [feminist adult education] potential to effect and consolidate substantive changes in women's lives is diminished' (Manicom & Walters, 1997, p. 71). Coming up the middle are assertions that these two elements are so inter-connected presenting them as a dichotomy or set of hierarchies is unhelpful (Walters & Manicom, 1996). I believe this more inter-connected argument is the most relevant in terms of an issue such as sexual exploitation where the pain is so personal and emotional yet bounded by and within a larger global patriarchal and capitalist framework. As demonstrated by the quilting project, connecting the emotional, political, practical, and strategic is where this fabric medium plays a valuable role.

Arts-based inquiry

Although by no means sharing the long history of feminist adult educa-tion, arts-based inquiry also arose as a challenge. It challenges the 'limit-ations and oppressive features of traditional scientific research, opening spaces for experimentation of alternative approaches . . . that weave aesthetic sensibilities and postpositivistic forms of expression' (Butter-wick, 2002, p. 243). Arts-based inquiry is essentially 'about writing outside of the lines, transgressing the rules, while staying within the lines of dominant discursive practices . . . [and is one of the] few ways we have left to disrupt the dominant discourses in society that silence and marginalise' (Ball, 2002, p. 2). The artistic representation created is 'the medium for messages needing to be heard' (Cole & McIntyre, 2004, p. 48).

This creative practice, however, has its challenges. For example, arts-based inquiry is most often associated with methods such as hermen-eutics, phenomenology, and autobiography as well as writing, fiction, journaling, self-narratives, and other language-based, discursive activities. A perusal of studies also shows that predominantly, arts-based inquiry focuses on the researcher exploring 'self' or the personal through an aesthetic medium (Dunlop, 2001). Even when arts-based inquiry is referred to as community-based, it is conducted most often 'for com-munity' and merely 'acknowledges the "everydayness" of knowledge construction and multiple ways of knowing' (Cole & McIntyre, 2004, p. 48). The products – the artworks, containing data, ways of knowing or representations of experience are created individually by the researchers based on their findings (Cole & McIntyre, 2004; Diamond, 1999; Dunlop, 2001).

Having said this, there are a few notable exceptions. As an art therapist, Ball (2002) uses a feminist framework and quilting as a research tool although she focuses on the personal. Feminist adult educator Butterwick (2002) uses popular theatre as a community-collaborative participatory research method for women to explore their 'experiences as feminists working in community and institutional contexts' (p. 240). In this chapter, I build on this arts-based research through an example of quilting as a medium for collaborative and collective arts-based inquiry 'with' women that both includes and moves beyond the therapeutic and local of sexual abuse.

The template: Sexual exploitation has no borders

To further contextualise this chapter within its diverse dimensions; sexual exploitation comes in a variety of forms ranging from incest to trafficking. It happens at home in the form of domestic abuse, in the workplace in the form of sexual harassment and on the streets where it includes everything from rape and homelessness to prostitution and sexual war crimes. Sexual exploitation is individual, personal, and localised. But it is also global, collective, and very political (Bain, Cranney, Delaney, Jiwani, Kler, Lakeman, Lewis, Odette, Spencer & Webb, 2006; DeKerseredy, Burshtyn & Gordon, 1995). Experiences of sexual violence and abuse are also deeply embedded in race (Bain *et al*, 2006).

Although sexual exploitation and abuse are keys issues for feminist adult educators, and in spite of efforts by 'women anti-violence activists, front-line shelter workers, women who have experienced violence, researchers and academics' to change the situation, they not only persist but actually seem to be increasing (Bain *et al*, 2006, p. 3; Fine, 1993). Across Canada, women's and family centres respond to the aftermath of exploitation and abuse through counselling, therapy, and safe havens. But equally importantly, they are beginning to respond to fundamental learning, knowledge, and research gaps by constructing 'creative . . . strategies to intervene and disrupt gendered and colonial forms of violence against women' (Bain *et al*, 2006, p. 3).

The learning, research and dissemination process

The *Sexual exploitation has no borders* quilting project was carried out in four phases, the last of which is ongoing. It was conceptualised and initiated by a family services centre on Vancouver Island in the province of British Columbia, Canada. I became involved with the centre's work through my research on women and the arts as well as my fabric craft connections to their celebrations of multiracial families.

The overall aim of the centre was to enhance and promote the quality and dignity of life for women, families, and groups within the community (Halsall & Ali, 2004). While much of the work is counselling and rehabilitation, there is a growing emphasis on collective, social learning and arts-based research. The quilt project was designed specifically to provide a medium and process through which women could collectively and imaginatively explore the very complex issue of sexual exploitation.

The central aim of this project was to create a combined educational and research process to uncover experiences and understandings of sexual exploitation from the standpoints of women who had suffered abuse and those who work with those women. It was decided from the outset the quilt would be used as a public education and knowledge dissemination tool, what I will refer to as phase four. The medium of quilting was chosen because everyone in the initial group at the centre seemed to have a natural interest in art as a form of expression and therefore, as Anne, the director and project creator and facilitator explained "creating a quilt with the participants just seemed natural".

The first phase was undertaken at the centre on Vancouver Island. The group of participants included six young women (youth) and social workers at the centre. The broad learning and research question framing the project and asked of each participant was: "What does sexual exploitation mean to you?" The women and girls were given squares of cloth approximately 10 x 10 centimetres. They also had at their disposal materials such as fabric paints, an assortment of buttons, old costume jewellery, ribbons as well as needles and thread. The diversity of materials meant those less adept with the needle could still contribute in a meaningful way. These squares were then transported for phase two across the Georgia Strait to the city of Vancouver on the lower mainland of British Columbia to the International Conference on Democracy and Citizenship (CIVICUS). CIVICUS is a global umbrella organisation that brings people together to promote active citizenship. Anne's group was invited to host a learning exchange based on the work around sexual exploitation.

Eighteen participants from North America, Africa, and Asia participated in the workshop. They were shown the designed squares by the group on Vancouver Island, provided with their own blank squares as well as all the other materials mentioned above, and were asked to respond to the same broad question. Of all the participants who completed their squares in both phases, six chose not to have theirs included in the final quilt. Some wanted to keep their squares (and this option was given at the beginning of the workshop) so they could duplicate the process in their own countries or centres while others "chose not to hand their squares in [because they] became too attached and squares were too personally meaningful" (Anne).

Phase three was sewing the stories, images, and ideas together: "now we had these powerful individual squares and stories but it was the putting them together that would make it the most meaningful. Here we were surrounded by scraps and we had to turn it into a quilt" (Anne). Jefferies (1998, p. 113) refers to this as a 'puzzle-picture', making, taking scraps of knowledge, meaning and experience and bringing them together in 'the overall texture of a quilt' to create a unified pattern and broader, more inter-woven understanding of an issue.

The squares ended up, since the centre had no sewing machine (sometimes it is just about practicality!), with a group of young women who belonged to a private sewing group. Initially, as Anne noted,

> I went to the class to use the machine and then given their interest, I worked them into the plan. They donated cloth from their projects to border the squares and as we sewed we talked. It was really quite unique because many of them did not know this stuff happened in Victoria.

With Anne's guidance, the group created the backing of the quilt and the placement of the various squares. As Anne's quotation above indicates, as the stories were sewn together the group obviously learned a great deal about the issue and the outcome is a beautiful, powerful, universal, and politicised work of fabric art.

As mentioned, phase four of this project was the dissemination of the collective learning and inquiry 'results' – the quilt. The overall goal of this very public exercise was to encourage further dialogue about the issue of sexual exploitation with different audiences. As it has turned out, those have included youth, academics, local, and international audiences. The quilt was first displayed at a local youth art show where it encountered something quite common to political and activist art: censorship (Felshin, 1995) and I address this through the appliqué. The quilt was also exhibited at two international events. The first was at an international adult education academic conference held at the University of Victoria in May 2004 where it took its place alongside many other works of art by women in Canada and around the world as part of my and my colleague, Joyce Stalker's, research work. The aim of the exhibition was to draw attention to women's arts and crafts as 'stimulants of imagination, spirit and dialogue, catalysts for personal, social, and environmental transformation, tools of justice, empowerment, and emancipation, and channels of energy, challenge and resistance' (Clover, 2004, p. ii). The second, again coming from our larger research work, was a large traditional quilt show held in Auckland, New Zealand in January 2005. Entitled *The Subversive Quilt*, the aim of our exhibition was to introduce women quilters to 'working media' that carried strong and vibrant messages of social justice. Currently the sexual exploitation quilt is on display with approximately 40 others at the Victoria October 2006 International Arts Symposium, *Artists of Conscience*.

Imagery in the quilt

Through words, image, design, colour, and symbol, the quilt is a tapestry through the making of emotion and cognition, local and international, personal and political, imagination and energy. The background of the quilt is a deep, dark fuchsia and there are sixteen squares in total. Some of the images focus on the personal/individual of sexual exploitation. For example, on one square, there is the figure of a tiny girl falling juxtaposed with a phoenix emerging from the ashes. Its aim was to express the complex simultaneous victim-agency feelings victims of sexual exploitation often have: falling/diminishing, and emerging/strengthening (DeKerseredy, Burshtyn & Gordon, 1995). Another carries an image of a little girl hidden by a black tassel. It reads 'little girls are hidden away by the shadow of everyday life.' While the image itself is extremely powerful, the story is even more so. Anne explained that a counsellor had identified this little girl as being on the periphery of being sexually exploited, but she had never spoken of it. Making this square enabled her to do so for the first time. Another square carries a single painted red splotch on black that the quilter said symbolised her pain. There are a number of others that carry images of black clouds and black smudges. A final image is an obviously pregnant woman lying with her legs apart and her vagina exposed.

One extremely fascinating image that at first does not appear to fit with the others but in fact serves a key purpose in terms of furthering a dialogue is a little symbol, one that aptly captures the complexity and political nature of the debates around sexual exploitation. It is a single large question mark and is just what it appears to be, a question. The young woman who created this image decided to approach the research question with her own provocative question: "What is sexual exploitation really all about?" She argued that although people say that it is wrong to have sex for money, she questioned whether "everyone" thought it was wrong. For example, men buy sex all the time. They pull up to kerbs looking for prostitutes with child car seats in the back. Do they think it is wrong? Creating spaces where provocative and re-formulated questions like this one can be asked as part of learning and research are extremely important in terms of more deeply exploring and connecting with an issue.

There are other squares that augment this political, learning journey. One entitled *He Promised* has two glittering rhinestone earrings attached. They immediately conjure an image of wealth and the good life. The words too seem positive: love, power, travel, safety, status, happiness, support, money and so on. But, according to the quilter, these are the "false riches dangled before young women in order to coax them into prostitution". Another linked square carries a chart with six little boxes depicting one progression into exploitation: 1) you are on the street; 2) you then go to discos and parties; 3) you have sex; 4) you need a place to stay, you need money and you need food; 5) you are abused; 6) you are trafficked to Japan, Korea, China or Singapore and you end up with HIV/AIDS. While at first it appears linear, in fact, you can read up and down, across and diagonally to see that you can simply move from one place to another and still end up in a difficult place. A final square addresses an even broader dimension of the sexual exploitation debate. It contains a bathing suit and a dress and it reads *The Need for Cool, Sexy Clothes*. It addresses negative socially-constructed body images and the fashion industry, both of which are considered to be a major a source of female exploitation (Rudman & Verdi, 1993; Stalker, 2003).

Appliqué: Quilting, feminist adult education and arts-based inquiry

Although numerous aspects of this project make thought-provoking and dynamic contributions to discourses of feminist adult education and arts-based inquiry, I will concentrate on only a few. Before doing so, however, I acknowledge these are primarily my thoughts, my analyses, my interpretations, my impressions and therefore, they can only ever be partial and subjective. Undoubtedly, they raise more questions than they actually answer.

The first aspect of the quilting project I find fascinating is its ability to provoke aesthetic oppositional messages and counter-messages that creatively, through design, colour, and image, destabilise fixed ideas and highlight complexities and dichotomies. Textiles broadly speaking are unique and a quite dichotomous medium. Bachmann and Scheuing (1998) suggest they are at one and the same time 'ubiquitous, banal, luxurious, celebrated, and diverse' (p. 15). Quilting in particular, is 'firmly rooted in the popular imagination as . . . one of the "gentle arts" usually associated with women' (Bachmann, 1998, p. 25). They are associated with comfort, warmth, security and the familiar (Halsall & Ali, 2004). Working with fabrics responds to the legitimate calls by feminist adult educators for safe, comfortable learning spaces that are caring and nurturing (Heng, 1996). The softness of the fabric, the familiarity, and the intimations of domesticity are comforting and known. But in the world of sexual exploitation, safety and comfort are often an illusion. This project (and many other quilt projects I encountered through my research) takes this so-called 'gentle' medium and turns it on its head, as the artist educator noted. So while the shape and construction suggest something in particular, the narrative images and colours tell a very different story. The quilt becomes a comforting and inviting yet brilliantly almost repelling juxtaposition of the conventional (properly quilted) with the unconventional (the critical stories) thereby providing an opportunity to perceive something on and of an object that is not part of the ordinary experience of that object (Young, 2001).

The complexity of this tool provoked multi-layered and multi-dimensional reflections. For example, within the border of the quilt there is one unified story but there are also several different levels or types of stories. The 'one story' is a collective presentation and analysis of violence against women. It is a voice of commonality, solidarity, of women united worldwide against abuse. But there are also individual voices where women attest to the 'subjectivity' of violence and abuse. Visually we see the emotional, local, and personal aspects which highlight the practical needs of sexually exploited women juxtaposed with the very collective, and global nature of the problem as expressed around global trafficking and HIV/AIDS – the strategic need to understand the politics of sexual exploitation. The quilt therefore responds to calls by feminist adult educators for a balance of personal and strategic as a disruptive art form that challenges injustice, allows for diversity, moves 'beyond narratives of victimization and otherness', and creates possibilities for broadened political discussions and a sense of togetherness (Sajinani & Nadeau, 2006).

Being encouraged to take risks and challenge oneself and others in learning is essential to any practice of transformative and critical learning (Ecclestone, 2004). Obviously, risk and challenge in this project come from simply discussing cross-culturally the very volatile issue of sexual exploitation. But they also come through the creation, design, or make-up of the quilt in two ways. First, challenge or risk in learning comes from being encouraged to be creative. This is not as easy as it sounds. Williamson (1998) has found that for many adults 'creativity has been thoroughly tamed and disenchanted' (p. 136). For a variety of reasons, they have a very impoverished sense of their own creative possibilities. What became clear is that the artist–educator had pushed the participants to take creative risks and be not only the researched, the researchers, and the knowers, but also, artists. Participants were valued not just for what they knew about the issue, but for their creativity and imaginations. Throughout my research, I have been surprised to find just how important recapturing the creative sense of self and being acknowledged as creative beings is to women. It is in being and becoming activist artists, something they never assumed themselves to be, where a valuable form of empowerment emerges: actors and agents of cultural and social change.

Second, in terms of risk and challenge in learning, we can look to colour and how this worked through the quilt. Colour is a crucial component of an art object's compositionality even when it is a black-and-white photograph (Rose, 2001). But colour in society is not neutral and neither is colour in the quilt. Fuchsia was chosen for the quilt frame because it is a combination of purple and red. As Anne stated, "purple represents the provincial colour for violence prevention and red represents the red light district. I also see purple as the colour of power and red as the colour of blood/violence". Going further, darker colours in the world of painting are assigned a lesser value than lighter ones (Rose, 2001). This is analogous to society where colour has been constructed in terms of good, happy, bold (white) and negative, inferior, bad (black). Many of the more personal images of pain, horror, and suffering in the quilt were black. This in fact sparked a debate at the CIVICUS conference as women challenged this choice. Although it is changing slowly, there have been legitimate critiques levelled at feminists because race is simply not fully understood in terms of its place in women's struggles (hooks, 1994). It is therefore, critical for feminist adult educators, when dealing with the gendered nature of sexual exploitation, to find ways to deal with the racialised aspect of this issue (Sajinani & Nadeau, 2006). Using colour is an alternative way to do this because it exposes the conscious and unconscious biases of society by making them visually apparent. Colour in the quilt becomes the interstice between things concrete and things abstract. As Anne herself noted, "it was pretty effective. It struck me just how many words we use [in English] without thinking; like black magic, or black mood".

The images accompanying the stories told by the participants can also be seen in terms of value added to learning. Pictures, images and symbols, like stories, also inform us. In fact, as Aristotle once argued, "the soul never thinks without a mental image" (in Manguel, 2002, p. 7). We are in fact surrounded by images in our homes as well as on the streets and through the media. Interestingly, Freire, in his early work on literacy in Brazil, asked his friend and well-known artist, Francisco Brennand, to draw a series of pictures that could be used to stimulate discussions about nature and culture . . . By the time the group had reached the tenth picture [they] had regained enormous confidence in themselves, pride in their culture, and a desire to learn more (Brown, 1974, p. 246–251).

Freire then asked the participants to create their own pictures in terms of how they understood the interconnection between culture and nature, and this led to a discussion of broader topics, more political topics such as 'people's resistance to change' (p. 250). A similar dynamic comes into play with quilts. There were many images in this quilt and others I have seen that cause this same capacity to evoke resistance. One is clearly the black images and symbols that exposed a way of creating and sharing 'meaning', as problematic. Another is the modest little symbol of the question mark that goes to the heart of the complex relationship within society of patriarchy, power, sexuality, and economics. Here we have an ontologically provocative space that resists pat answers. The falsity of the power and wealth of prostitution is visually glaring in the rhinestone earrings. Storied images, whether we are directly affected by an issue or not, allow us the creative freedom to construct our own narratives, never final or bound to either one interpretation or subject (Brown, 1974; Manguel, 2002).

Another aspect of this project that is dynamic is its contribution to the process-versus-product debates in feminist adult education, research, and arts-based inquiry (Butterwick, 2002; Butterwick & Dawson, 2006; Lather, 1991). Most often arts and adult education "are considered in two dimensions: art as process (the act of making) and art as product (the resulting work)" (Butterwick, 2006, p. 286). In feminist 'praxis-oriented research, reciprocally-educative process is more important than the product as empowering methods contribute to consciousness' (Lather, 1991, p. 72). Moreover, often the artwork is simply seen as the 'expressive medium [used] to investigate problems' (*ibid.*, p. 245) rather than a primary force in the research. There are many reasons why process is of vital importance. Art works such as this quilt do not emerge from 'a vacuum and looking at them for what they are runs the risk of neglecting the ways in which they were produced and interpreted' (Rose, 2001, p. 37). But much can be gained from seeing process and product together as a 'holistic approach to learning and inquiry' (Butterwick, 2006, p. 282). Processes are metaphors in their own right, 'powerful containers of meaning' which means that 'looking at the product at the end, or looking only at the social good intentions . . . is certainly not the whole picture' (Kelly in McGauley, 2006, p. 45). The quilt project was created for those involved to learn and engage in a research process, but the quilt itself was meant to be a dialogic aesthetic in the public domain. There was an underlying assumption that the dialogue of the process would be picked up again through audience interaction with the artwork, a provocative latency of a process, which begins with the transposition of aesthetic experience into symbolic or communicative action (McGauley, 2006). Adding to this, Felshin (1995) discusses how shoddy collective, activist artwork is often dismissed as amateurish and the message as well as the relationships and process are lost. That both quality and visibility have to be taken into account in terms of public and collective arts must in some way become a given. I came to realise just what Felshin meant in terms of quality during the traditional quilt show in Auckland where we presented the sexual exploitation and other social justice-oriented quilts. Women quilters from around the world hesitantly approached the quilts and only relaxed and read the message after they recognised the quality of the work. They touched the seams, turned the quilts over, and did a thorough investigation of the 'craft'. The sexual exploitation quilt is indeed a well-crafted piece of activist art and a tactile visual representation of the multiple realities of sexual exploitation in which its creators can take great pride and audiences appreciate. Now one can argue that quality simply propels us into an art world of elitism and should be disregarded, but if one in fact agrees with the adult education principle of beginning where people are at, it does become relevant. The quilters in New Zealand expected a certain quality of craftwork and finding it meant opening up to new possibilities as one woman commented: "This quilt is so beautifully done. I'm a quilter and that is why I came here [to exhibit] . . . This quilt comes from Canada, but these issues, well, it could just as easily be done here." Perhaps we could argue the best collective works of political or activist art are those with 'one foot in the art world and the other, in the world of political activism' (Felshin, 1995, p. 9)?

Adding to this discussion, Lippard (1984) suggests that artworks are not 'effective simply by being created, but by being . . . communicated' (p. 5). When created for public distribution, an artwork in fact remains an active educative tool long after the initial process has ended. And as I make my way through exhibitions and listen to the women who come to view this quilt, I hear them discuss what the images mean and make their own meanings. Perhaps even more importantly, the women who created the quilt can simply sit back and watch as it dares to make publicly explicit their ideas around ingrained sexism in society. They were protected, anonymous, yet in fact are speaking out loudly through this provocative, conflictual, and somewhat disarming little piece of fabric. And often political art is meant to be controversial, to provoke debate, and yes, as Overton (1994) reminds us, can 'cause outrage and indignation' (p. 89). That art sometimes seeks to provoke and outrage can often result in censorship. When Anne put the quilt on display as part of a youth art show held at her centre, "the quilt remained folded over for the whole time! I was told that some of the youths' parents would find it offensive and there was not really room for discussion about it". Ball (2002) argues that using arts-based methodologies may be risky, but it is a very important struggle and one we should not abandon simply because instances of censorship occur. While censorship is problematic in one way, in another, one can take pride in the fact that it must have been a very effective little piece of fabric indeed to have been found so controversial and then silenced. Adding to this, although it was silenced in one venue, it spoke loudly and clearly at an international arts conference in October 2006, in downtown Victoria.

Conclusion

As a research project, this quilt is a collective and participatory project and not an individual endeavour. Having said this I am in no way suggesting all arts-based research should be collective and that creations by researchers are not powerful. One need only see the Alzheimer Arts exhibition by adult educators Ardra Cole and Maura McIntyre (2006) to realise this is not so. However, a fundamental of feminist adult education and research is to make the world a better, more just place for women by placing the power of exploration and learning in their hands. From start to finish, the women were involved in data collection, analysis, construction, and presentation. This quilt, metaphorically speaking, takes the basic fabric of their knowledge from the past and weaves it into a tapestry through the making – a comforter of collective construction and mobilisation of knowledge. Ball (2002, p. 19) believes that 'in order to know' researchers must be connected but also 'committed to the development of different ways of knowing through the development of different methodologies such as arts-based methodologies'. For me, in order to truly 'write outside the lines', as Ball suggested, researchers must also be willing to let go of the art as their own product, representation, and way of knowing and be able to see the power in collective production. Perhaps this leads us back to the issue of quality, but as this quilt shows, quality comes not just from the artist-researcher, but from the women researchers involved who are allowed to be artists.

This quilting project is an inter-related phenomenon of process and product; a discursive formation from which many meanings emerge (Perron, 1998). Process is about developing, building, facilitating, and following; the artwork is a metaphor for that relationship, representing the space where that particular conversation ended. Both process and product contain complex layers of meaning, of learning, of emotion, of politics, of relationships of experience merging and emerging through words, imagery, and symbol. The quilt visually represents the multiple, local and international realities of sexual exploitation, a tactile testament to creativity, survival, and power that endures in the sound of rustling fabric. What I have learned is that quilting is a vibrant, fluid, and complex form of feminist adult education that lends itself easily to a more participatory and inclusive practice of knowledge creation, presentation and dissemination. Now all I need to do is learn to sew!

References

Bachmann, I. (1998) 'Material and the promise of the immaterial'. In I. Bachmann & R. Scheuing (eds), *Materials matters: The art and culture of contemporary textiles* (pp. 23–34). Toronto: YYZ Books.

Bain, B., Cranney, B., Delaney, D., Jiwani, Y., Kler, D., Lakeman, L., Lewis, S., Odette, F., Spencer L. and Webb, A. (2006) 'Editorial', *Canadian Women Studies*, Vol. 25, Nos. 1&2, p. 3.

Ball, H. K. (2002) 'Subversive materials: Quilts as social text', *Alberta Journal of Educational Research*, Vol. 60, No. 3, pp. 1–27.

Bart, P. and Moran, E.G. (1993) *Violence against women: The bloody footprints*. Newbury Park, Ca. USA: Sage Publications.

Brown, C. (1974) 'Literacy in thirty hours: Paulo Freire's process', *The Urban Review*, Vol. 7, No. 3, pp. 245–56.

Butterwick, S. (2002) 'Your story/my story/our story: Performing interpretation in participatory theatre', *Alberta Journal of Educational Research*, Vol. 60, No. 3, pp. 240–53.

Butterwick, S. and Dawson, J. (2006) 'Adult education and the arts'. In T. Fenwick, T. Nesbit and B. Spencer (eds.), *Context of adult education: Canadian perspectives* (pp. 281–92). Toronto: Thompson Educational Publishing.

Clover, D. E. (ed) (2004) 'Adult education for democracy, social justice and a culture of peace'. *Proceedings of the 23rd annual conference of the Canadian Association for the Study of Adult Education*. Victoria, B.C.: University of Victoria.

Clover, D. E. and Stalker, J. (eds) (2005) 'Arts, social justice and adult education', *Convergence*, Vol. 38, No. 4.

Clover, D. E., Stalker, J. and McGauley, L. (2004) 'Feminist Popular Education and Community Leadership: The Case for New Directions'. In D. E. Clover (ed), 'Adult education for democracy, social justice and a culture of peace', *Proceedings of the 23rd annual conference of the Canadian Association for the Study of Adult Education*, pp. 89–94. Victoria, B.C.: University of Victoria.

Cole, A. and McIntyre, M. (2004) 'Arts-informed research for public education: The Alzheimer's Project', *Proceedings of the 22nd Annual Conference of the Canadian Association for the Study of Adult Education* (pp. 45–50). Halifax: Dalhousie University/University of King's College.

Cole, A. and McIntyre, M. (with Burns, L.) (2006) *Living and dying with dignity: The Alzheimer's project*. Halifax: Backalong Books.

DeKerseredy, W., Burshtyn, H. and Gordon, C. (1995) 'Taking women abuse seriously: A critical response to the Solicitor General of Canada's Crime Prevention Advice'. In E. D. Nelson and B. W. Robinson (eds),

Gender in the 1990s: Images, realities and issues (pp. 478–89). Toronto: Nelson Canada.

Diamond, C.T.P. and Mullen, C. (1999) *The postmodern educator: Arts-based inquiries and teacher development*. New York: Peter Lang.

Doerge, S. (1992) *Feminist popular education: Transforming the world from where women stand*. Unpublished paper.

Dunlop, R. (2001) 'Excerpts from Boundary Bay: A novel as educational research'. In A. L. Neilsen, A. Cole and J. G. Knowles (eds) *The Art of Writing Inquiry* (pp. 11–25). Halifax, Nova Scotia: Backalong Books.

Ecclestone, K. (2004). 'Season's readings', *Adults Learning*, p. 21, December.

Felshin, N. (1995) *But is it art?: The spirit of art as activism*. Seattle: Bay Press.

Fine, M. (1993) 'The politics of research and activism: Violence against women'. In B. Bart and E. G. Moran (eds) *Violence against women: The bloody footprints* (pp. 278–87). Newbury Park, Ca. USA: Sage Publications Inc.

Halsall, E. and Ali, S. (2004) 'Unravelling quilted texts: An alternate inquiry into the social fabric of life', *Journal of Child and Youth Care Work*, Vol. 17, No. 1, pp. 136–140.

Heng, C. L. (1996) 'Talking pain: educational work with factory women in Malaysia'. In S. Walters and L. Manicom (eds) *Gender in Popular Education* (pp. 202–228). London: Zed Books.

hooks, b. (1994) *Teaching to transgress, education as the practice of freedom*. New York and London: Routledge.

Horsman, J. (2000) *Too scared to learn. Women, violence and education*. London: Lawrence Erlbaum.

Jefferies, J. (1998) 'Autobiographical patterns'. In I. Bachmann and R. Scheuing (eds) *Materials matters: the art and culture of contemporary textiles* (pp. 107–20). Toronto: YYZ Books.

Jongeward, C. (1994) 'Connecting with creative process: Adult learning through art making within a supportive community', *Proceedings of the 13th annual conference of the Canadian Association for the Study of Adult Education: Theory and practice* (pp. 237–42). Vancouver: Simon Fraser University.

Lacy, S. (1995) *Mapping the terrain: New genre public art.* Seattle: Bay Press.

Lather, P. (1991) *Getting smart feminist research and pedagogy with/in the postmodern.* New York: Routledge.

Lippard, L. (1984) *Get the message? A decade of art for social change.* New York: Dutton, Inc.

Manguel, A. (2002) *Reading pictures.* Toronto: Vintage Canada.

Manicom, L. and Walters, S. (1997) 'Feminist popular education in light of globalization'. In S. Walters (ed) *Globalization, adult education and training: Impacts and issues.* London: Zed Books.

McGauley, L. (2006) *Utopian languages: Romanticism, subversion and democracy in community arts.* Unpublished Master of Arts thesis, Laurentian University, Sudbury, Ontario.

Overton, P. (1994) 'The role of community arts development in nurturing the invisible culture of rural genius'. *From artspeak to artaction: Proceedings of a community arts development conference* (pp. 87–97). Saskatoon: University of Saskatchewan.

Perron, M. (1998) 'Common threads: Local strategies for inappropriated artists'. In I. Bachmann and R. Scheuing (eds) *Materials matters: The art and culture of contemporary textiles* (pp. 121–36). Toronto: YYZ Books.

Rose, G. (2001) *Visual methodologies.* London: Sage Publications.

Rudman, W. J. and Verdi, P. (1993) 'Exploitation: comparing sexual and violent imagery of females and males in advertising', *Women Health*, Vol. 20, No. 4, pp. 1–14.

Sajinani, N. and Nadeau, D. (2006) 'Creating safer spaces for immigrant women of colour', *Canadian Women's Studies*, Vol. 25, Nos. [1&2), pp. 45–52.

Stalker, J. (2003) 'Ladies' work and popular education: Fabricating new approaches', *New Zealand Journal of Adult Education*, Vol. 31, No. 2, pp. 21–35.

Stalker, J. (2004) 'Stylish women: Learning, fashion and identity formation'. In D. Clover (ed), *Adult education for democracy, social justice and a culture of peace, Proceedings of the 45th Adult Education Research Conference* (pp. 456–61). Victoria, BC: University of Victoria.

Thompson, J. (1997) *Words in edgeways: Radical learning for social change.* Leicester: NIACE.

Walters, S. (1997) *Globalization, adult education and training.* London: Zed Books.

Walters, S. and Manicom, L. (1996) *Gender in popular education.* London: Zed Books.

Williamson, B. (2004). *Lifeworlds and learning.* Leicester: NIACE.

Young, J. (2001) *Art and knowledge.* New York, Routledge.

Section Three

Arts-based adult learning
and democracy

CHAPTER 5

Voyeurism, consciousness–raising, empowerment

Opportunities and challenges of using legislative theatre to 'practise democracy'

Catherine Etmanski

Introduction

Theatre is a long-established means of re/presenting reality. Through the theatre, actors, directors, spectators and outside critics – whether professional or amateur – collaborate in reflecting upon, interpreting, portraying, and potentially changing certain aspects of the human condition. In this sense, the theatre, like other art forms, is innately political in its capacity to maintain the status quo or to transform our perceptions of reality. Not only because audience perceptions of reality can be transformed, but also because people will act upon those newly-formed perceptions, many agents of social change, including educators, have adapted theatre techniques to accomplish socially-oriented goals (Boal, 1979, 1998; Butterwick, 2002, 2003; Prentki & Selman, 2000). The practice of 'popular theatre' has thus emerged in conjunction with the global adult and popular education movement to become a powerful tool of reflection, consciousness-raising, empowerment and, at its best, of mobilising personal and collective action against oppressive social systems.

This chapter gives the account of one popular theatre process in Vancouver, Canada: Headlines Theatre's *Practicing Democracy* project.

Inspired by the 'legislative theatre' (LT) work of Brazilian educator and director Augusto Boal (1998), this city-wide production was the first documented attempt at using theatre to create legislation in Canada. In giving this account of the *Practicing Democracy* project, my goal is to share some important insights on LT, both with those who are unfamiliar with this concept, and with educators and other agents of social change who already know its power and potential.

I begin by introducing the concept of popular theatre through a review of literature. I then detail the process of completing the *Practicing Democracy* project, and go on to list some of the opportunities and challenges of using popular theatre to 'practise democracy'. Finally, following Boal (1979) and Prentki and Selman (2000), I debate a theoretical question around the intended audience(s) for public popular theatre productions. Perceived and real differences and similarities in social positioning between audience members and actors, I demonstrate, can lead to divergent actor and audience experiences: from voyeurism, to consciousness-raising, to empowerment.

The data I draw upon for this chapter are based on a pilot case study for a larger research project. I conducted the first round of data collection in March 2004 in conjunction with an 'Action-Oriented Research' seminar at the University of Victoria. This time period corresponded with Headlines' public performances of the play *Practicing Democracy*. This initial study included seven interviews with two representatives from Headlines, four audience members, and one Vancouver City Councillor. It also included participant observation as an audience member during four performances of the play. Follow-up research occurred between March 2004 and August 2005, during which time I corresponded with Headlines' staff, primarily with David Diamond (the Artistic Director) who also reviewed this manuscript. I attended a smaller-scale performance of a subsequent Headlines play as well, and conducted a document review of final reports, media releases, and other texts available through the Headlines Theatre website. In addition, I attended a six-day professional development training course with Headlines, where I developed an experiential understanding of the principles of popular theatre through hands-on practice.

Introduction to popular theatre

Popular theatre is a dynamic art form, with multiple, culturally-determined uses. It can combine dramatic techniques with song, dance, and body movement; with personal narrative, storytelling, rhythm and percussion; with puppetry, costumery, masks and other local innovations, all serving to activate the heart and body in order to engage both participants and potential audiences alike (Boal, 1979, 1998, 2002; Legarda, 2002; Plastow & Tsehaye, 1998; Steward, 1970). The drama itself can be performed either privately for a group's own purpose, or before an audience in theatres, classrooms, or on makeshift stages: in the streets, on the metro, in parks, or under shady baobab trees (Boal, 1979, 1998; Byam, 1999; Gallagher, 2001; Steward, 1970). It can provide a space for personal reflection and transformation (Nelson, 1993), a means of building solidarity (Butterwick, 2003), a process of community development (Hinsdale, Lewis & Waller, 1995), or a venue to propose new legislation (Boal, 1998). In its most common understanding, popular theatre is theatre made by the people, for the people.

Since theatre in its various manifestations exists in most societies around the world, drawing rigid boundaries around what is and what is not popular theatre becomes an endeavour with questionable intentions. Nevertheless, allow me to clarify this broad definition by beginning with a discussion of what it is not. Prentki and Selman (2000) draw attention to a natural confusion that occurs for those unfamiliar with this concept, one that stems from connotations of the word 'popular' in the English-speaking world. They explain that popular does not necessarily mean that 'a lot of people attend' (p. 9), although that may be true of some popular theatre performances. Mainstream or well-attended middle- and upper-class theatre performances (Prentki and Selman give the example of mega-musicals) are what Boal (1998) refers to as 'populist' theatre – theatre consumed by the masses.

Popular theatre, then, is not merely a form of passive entertainment that reproduces the status quo; it is theatre with a goal of social change. It generally has a subversive intent, and can also be used for community organising or educational purposes. In essence, the term:

> Implies that the process of making and showing the theatre piece is
> owned and controlled by a specific community, that the issues and

> stories grow out of the community involved, and that the community
> is a vital part of a process of identifying, examining and taking action
> on matters which that community believes need to change.
>
> (Prentki and Selman, 2000, p. 9)

The act of creating a popular theatre production can thus be described as an action-oriented participatory research process, whereby community members come together to share and analyse their own stories, make decisions around how best to represent those stories, and then disseminate them by means of the theatre. 'The people' or the community members in question can refer to either a geographic community, or one with shared interests, whether it be individuals belonging to the same labour union (Prentki & Selman, 2000), living in the same remote fishing village (Filewod, 1998), or sharing the social label of 'teenage moms' (Nelson, 1993).

Various theatre movements exist around the world, for example the 'Theatre for Development' movement across the African continent (Byam, 1999; Manyozo, 2002; Mda, 1993) and the 'Theatre in Schools' movement throughout the UK (Ball, 1995; Prentki & Selman, 2000). Theatre's historical connection with politics is likewise well documented. Referring to Western conceptions of democracy, Gillespie (1995) highlights the integral role theatre played in the public life of Ancient Greece, with the content of plays 'routinely grappling with the pressing political and philosophical issues of the day' (p. 100). While this particular form of democracy and political theatre would probably not have included the participation of women and slaves, this example nevertheless demonstrates a link between the roots of democracy and theatre.

Other theorists have written about the theatre's potential for social commentary in more (overtly) politically oppressive times. As Obeyesekere (1999) explains, in 1978, when the authoritarian Jayawardene government came to power in Sri Lanka, 'the theatre became a kind of open forum for the popular dissatisfaction that could not find expression elsewhere in society' (p. 50). Likewise, the founding members of the Philippine Educational Theatre Association (PETA) saw it as their social responsibility to use theatre as an educational medium to oppose the Marcos dictatorship (Legarda, 2002).

Canadians, too, have a rich tradition of using theatre for political purposes. In her account of the development of popular theatre in

Canada, Selman (2000) draws a connection between the emergence of multiple theatre companies during the late 1960s and 1970s and the parallel push for a nationwide Canadian identity during this time. In opposition to imported theatre productions from Great Britain and the United States, local communities began researching and performing their own histories in what came to be known as 'collective documentaries'. While the content of these documentaries was not overtly subversive in and of itself, Selman writes that in telling truly Canadian stories and elevating 'our citizens, our neighbours, to the stage' (p. 74), this type of theatre was indeed a form of cultural resistance.

The legacy of Augusto Boal

While it is true that political theatre has been used in many parts of the world, the 'Theatre of the Oppressed' work of Brazilian director and educator Augusto Boal (1979) has undeniably had a strong influence on the theory and practice of popular theatre. Two of Boal's (1998) concepts are particularly relevant to the *Practicing Democracy* project: 'forum' and 'legislative' theatre. As with most popular theatre, in forum theatre a play is constructed around the issues most pressing to the community at work. The protagonists in the play, however, always encounter oppressive situations in which they lose. When it comes time to perform the piece publicly, it is performed once in its entirety and then replayed a second time from the beginning. During the second performance, audience members are invited to yell "Stop!" at any time and come on stage to replace a character with whose struggle they can identify. When they do come on stage, these audience members try to change the outcome of events so that the character, in changing her or his behaviour, can also change the outcome of the oppressive interaction. Not all interventions are successful, which means that community members can use theatre not only to imagine solutions to their problems, but also to investigate the feasibility of the solutions offered by audience interventions.

However, we know that many oppressive situations are caused by oppressive structures (laws, policies, ideologies, etc.), not only by individuals. In recognising the limitations of individual agency in the face of these structures, Boal (1998) seized an opportunity to begin an experiment in what he terms 'legislative' theatre (LT). After spending over 20 years in exile, Boal was (surprisingly) elected as a Vereador (City Councillor) when he returned to Rio de Janeiro, Brazil in 1992. In this position of relative power, he was able to begin using the theatre to explore popular concerns and transform the people's desires into law. During his three years in office, Boal managed to pass 13 municipal laws and then went on to carry out further experiments in Munich and Paris. Boal continues to encourage experimentation with LT around the world. Indeed, it is this experiment in using theatre to make law that recently spread to Canada through the work of Headlines Theatre.

Theatre for Living

Headlines Theatre is a non-profit theatre company based in Vancouver, Canada. Founded in 1981 by a group of local artists, Headlines' main focus at that time was 'Agit-Prop' (Agitation Propaganda) theatre about political issues of concern to Vancouver communities. When David Diamond, who had worked with Boal, became the new Artistic Director in 1984, Headlines' focus changed from theatre for communities to theatre with communities. Headlines now provides a range of opportunities for people to become involved in theatre for social change. They offer training in Diamond's own approach to popular theatre, which he terms Theatre for Living (TFL), as well as a number of community events, including an annual main stage production (Headlines Theatre, 2005).

Without question, Diamond has been greatly influenced by his friend and colleague Augusto Boal. Like Boal, Diamond has drawn upon Paulo Freire's approach to critical education. However, while Boal's *Theatre of the Oppressed* is the foundation of TFL, Diamond's model is increasingly moving away from a binary oppressor/oppressed divide and is seeking to expose the complexity of power relationships in any situation of oppression. This shift began as a result of his work on issues of family violence with the United Native Nations in 1992. Before engaging in the work, community members had requested that the character of the abuser, or 'oppressor' 'be portrayed as a person who needed healing – not a criminal' (Diamond, 2004a, p. 5). According to Diamond, this demonstrated a difference between 'creating a character whose actions we do not condone and creating a character who we ridicule' (p. 5). In TFL, it is important to portray how the so-called oppressors can themselves be oppressed, or at least dealing with their own struggles, and how violence can at times be motivated by feelings of care or even love.

In addition to his university theatre training and his decades of work using theatre for community development, Diamond's TFL is also influenced by his hobby of studying quantum physics. He rejects the Cartesian mind/body dualism, the resulting conceptual division between humans and their ecosystems, and the failure of modern science to realise the interconnectedness of all matter in the universe. These beliefs come into play in TFL in his understanding of communities as living organisms: 'just as you are a collection of individual cells that make up your body, a community is a collection of individual people that make up the living organism of the community' (Diamond, 2004a, p. 8). He goes on to claim that if communities do not express themselves they get sick, just as individuals get sick if they repress their emotions. Theatre, he asserts, is a primal language that communities have long used as a means of self-expression; therefore, learning how to create rather than simply consume theatre (and other art forms) is one way to heal communities and work toward positive social change.

The *Practicing Democracy* process

While Headlines' productions always tackle important community issues, their first attempt at using the theatre to inform policy was during the 1999 production of *Squeegee*, a play produced in conjunction with homeless Vancouver youths. Headlines enlisted a legal advocate to attend the public performances, transcribe audience ideas and interventions into the forum, and transform those ideas into a legislative report. This report was subsequently presented to the Vancouver City Council, but unfortunately, Council members at that time refused to read the document. With this refusal the possibility of theatre influencing City policy seemed quashed (Headlines Theatre, 2005).

The Municipal elections of November 2002, however, brought about a significant change in Vancouver's City Council, with the majority of seats taken by members of the Coalition of Progressive Electors. As Diamond had a prior working relationship with several Councillors, he immediately proposed another LT process, and on 27 February 2003 a motion that Council endorse Headlines' proposed LT project was carried unanimously. With endorsement from the City securely in place, Headlines' staff members began their preparations for the *Practicing Democracy* project (Diamond, 2004b).

Four potential topics for the LT process were short-listed from recent City Council agendas and subsequently advertised through Headlines' extensive community networks and other forms of local media. Members of the public were asked to vote on which topic they would like to see addressed through the LT process. At that time, (March–April 2003) many Vancouver residents were concerned with a pending threat that the Provincial Government would impose a two-year time limit on access to Income Assistance (welfare), leaving thousands of British Columbians without the social safety net Canadians have worked hard to put in place. As a result, investigating how the City could respond to these attacks on social security was voted to be the most important topic to address (Diamond, 2004b). Due to public outrage and mass activism across the province, the Provincial Government rescinded its decision to impose this time limit during the preparatory period for the *Practicing Democracy* project. Headlines Theatre therefore modified its topic to address how the City of Vancouver could respond to years of Provincial cuts to social services.

During the following nine months (May 2003 to January 2004) Headlines prepared for the production. Thirty participants with lived experiences relating to Provincial Government cuts to social services were recruited to take part in a community workshop from which the script for the play would be written. Prior to this workshop, six of those 30 participants were selected to co-create and act in the final public performance. It is important to note here that Headlines insists on paying workshop participants for their involvement, and in this case enough funds were also raised to subsidise daycare for single parents, and to rent safe, temporary shelter for homeless participants. In this sense, participation in both the theatre workshop and the final production was not merely treated as an interesting artistic or therapeutic experience – it was work! This also meant that a vital part of the preparations included fundraising. Headlines calculates that based on the total project budget of $151,391 (Canadian dollars), each of the 18 performances cost approximately $8,411 (including salaries, theatre and equipment rental), while average donations at each performance were approximately $600. In short, this city-wide experiment in democracy was highly subsidised by Headlines (Diamond, 2004).

The 30-participant workshop was held between 1 February and

6 February 2004, during which time theatre games and techniques were used to tell the participants' stories of living the effects of Provincial cutbacks to social services. Immediately following this workshop, the six pre-selected cast members, in collaboration with Headlines staff, went to work writing the script. Here I will draw your attention to the short timeframe between the workshop and the opening night of 3 March 2004. Not only was this a quick timeline for the creation of a play, but also for the design and acquisition of a set that included props as small as a water glass and as large as a dumpster. This rapid play production is based on a six-day workshop Diamond has developed through his contractual work with communities around the world. He refers to this innovation as 'Power Plays', alluding to both the colloquial use of the word 'power' to mean quick but effective (c.f. power walk, power nap), as well as to the exploration of the 'power plays' or power dynamics that occur in communities and are reproduced during the workshop. Diamond (2004a) describes a Power Play as 'an intense process of group building, theatrical language learning, issue identification and exploration, play creation, and Forum Theatre performance' (p. 7). The end result of the Power Play workshop is a public performance of the community's play(s), as was the case with the six-member *Practicing Democracy* workshop.

The public performances of *Practicing Democracy* ran from 3 to 21 March 2004, with 18 shows in three locations. In order to ensure accessibility, admission was by donation and the locations were strategically chosen to encourage the attendance of Vancouver residents from various demographic backgrounds. The first week of performances was held at the Japanese Hall in Vancouver's Downtown Eastside: a vibrant community, but also one of Canada's poorest neighbourhoods. The second week was performed at the Croatian Cultural Centre in East Vancouver, in a predominantly working class and ethnically diverse neighbourhood. The final week was performed at St. James Community Square on the West side of Vancouver, an affluent neighbourhood and also the electoral district for the Provincial Premier under whose leadership time limits on access to welfare were proposed. Each theatre setting provided approximately 100 seats, and Headlines estimated an average of 72 per cent capacity per show. Furthermore, one show was televised via Shaw Community Television, which reached approximately 5,000 viewers. With these numbers, Headlines claimed that roughly

6,300 people viewed and participated in the *Practicing Democracy* project (Diamond, 2004b).

As described earlier, this LT project had the ultimate goal of producing policy recommendations that fell within Municipal jurisdiction. To assist in this process, Carrie Gallant, a Vancouver lawyer, had a similar responsibility of compiling audience ideas into a final report. This report contained 90 policy recommendations in the areas of 1) housing (e.g. women-only shelters, affordable housing); 2) support for target groups (e.g. seniors, sex trade workers); 3) economic opportunities (e.g. job creation and support for job maintenance); 4) food (e.g. systematic distribution of fruit from local trees); and 5) safety (e.g. watchdog legislation against police brutality) (Gallant, 2004). This report was completed on 21 April 2004 and presented to City Hall on 6 May 2004 (Diamond & Gallant, 2004).

By 15 September 2004 Council announced its official response to the *Practicing Democracy* project. This response comprised a report that detailed the City's mandate in each of the five areas of recommendation and described City initiatives already underway that mirrored recommendations in Gallant's report (City of Vancouver, 2004). While it is important that this time Council did in fact address the *Practicing Democracy* report, both Headlines Theatre staff and members of the general public protested that Council's response did not sufficiently recognise the depth and breadth of the process, nor did it adequately address the innovative recommendations that were included in the report. Thus, through extensive dialogue between Headlines Theatre and City Councillors, it was acknowledged that Council's report 'needed more work' (*Practicing Democracy* website, 2005). On 18 October 2004, Council removed its report from the agenda and committed to more thoroughly addressing Headlines' recommendations. To date, many recommendations have been reviewed in further detail, and in particular, steps have been taken toward creating a 'Homeless and Sex Trade Worker Advocate' position at the City of Vancouver (*Practicing Democracy*, 2005). At the time of writing this chapter – October 2005, two and a half years after the City of Vancouver's initial endorsement of the project – progress is slow, but the process is still underway.

Opportunities and challenges:
Insights from the research

While the idea of LT is attractive, as is evident from this account of the *Practicing Democracy* project, creating legislation using theatre is a time-consuming and potentially expensive process. Leaving aside the common constraints of time and money, I focus the following discussion on more nuanced practical and theoretical insights gained from this research. The practical insights are related to the LT process, and here I play with options that might better support the implementation phase of such projects. These practical concerns give rise to theoretical insights around the roles of actors and audience members, which have more abstract implications that practitioners are not likely to resolve simply by changing the process.

The legislative theatre process: Practical insights

As is common with many public consultation processes, and as appears to be the case with this project, major hurdles arise during the policy implementation phase. While Augusto Boal had the advantage of being a Vereador in Rio de Janeiro and could therefore more readily implement laws made under his direction, Headlines had no such advantage. Although it was hoped and believed that the City's endorsement of the project would ultimately lead to the implementation of several recommendations from the final report, there can be no such guarantee on behalf of a City and indeed, it appears that there was not a universal understanding about what this initial endorsement entailed.

Several obstacles between Council endorsement and the implementation phase are worth noting here. Midway through the preparations for this project Diamond encountered one Councillor in public who inquired about Headlines' current projects. Although he recalled, 'watch[ing] this man raise his hand and vote in support of the project!' (Diamond, 2004b, p. 9), Diamond re-explained *Practicing Democracy* to this Councillor, who nodded his approval. Diamond later conceded that since Council endorses hundreds of new projects weekly, Councillors cannot be expected to remember the details of each one. Through this encounter he learned the important lesson that it is his responsibility to provide frequent reminders and updates to Council about the project, and when it came time for the public showing of *Practicing Democracy*, a personal invitation was sent to each Councillor. Unfortunately, only six of the 11 Councillors attended the play. The others were given a video copy of the televised evening and requested to view it before Headlines' report was submitted to Council. As attending and participating in a forum theatre performance is a unique aesthetic experience that can provoke an emotional and physical, as well as intellectual response, it is difficult to know whether the Councillors who did not witness the live process completely appreciated the depth or power of this type of community dialogue.

It is evident that a mechanism for clarifying all participants' roles and responsibilities around implementation should be included at the outset of any future experimentation with LT. There should also be a process for ensuring that all Councillors view the forum theatre in action. Incidentally, the Vancouver City Council did make Headlines an offer to allow the group to perform a 5 to 10 minute skit in the Council Chamber. Diamond refused this offer, arguing that the art that was the final product – including the lighting, props, digitally-projected images, sound, and staging – would have been undermined in such a short representation:

> The suggestion to do [a short skit] is a suggestion to have done a completely different project. The power of the project comes from it having been, I think, very good theatre that worked on all the levels that theatre works. I INSIST that when we do main stage projects we make the best art we can, because I believe that it is through the creation of powerful art that change occurs. I have seen way too many 'socially relevant plays' that have great politics but are lacking in artistry. (Personal communication, 19 January 2005, emphasis in original)

That said, if City Councillors cannot commit to attending the scheduled performances, perhaps a special showing for the Council could occur. The 30 workshop participants could also be invited to attend and participate in the forum alongside the Councillors. This format might encourage creative dialogue between Councillors and the people whose needs they are aiming to address, or it would at least be an opportunity for the actors (and the people whose stories they are acting) to have their stories heard by Council.

Finally, while acknowledging the goodwill on behalf of Councillors through their willingness to experiment with a new kind of public consultation, this did not (and did not intend to) fundamentally alter the process by which laws are changed and new legislation is enacted. Neither did it radically alter power relations between people affected by cuts to social services (i.e. workshop participants) and those who have control over of the policies that affect their lives (i.e. Councillors and Provincial Members of the Legislative Assembly). While participants and actors may have felt empowered throughout this process, the decision-making power still remains in the hands of Councillors. This project therefore highlights some of the difficulties Canada's most marginalised citizens face in having their voices heard and their needs addressed – even through such a creative approach to democracy.

Voyeurism, consciousness-raising, empowerment: Theoretical insights

The above challenges surrounding the implementation of policy recommendations raise, for me, a question around the roles of actors and audience members in a LT process. I would therefore like to present a philosophical debate that may have practical implications for those interested in using theatre for social change. If the primary goal of a LT process is to make structural change, should the audience be limited to those with a direct understanding of the issue and those with the power or desire to work toward that change? Or is social change such a subtle concept that anyone should have a right to participate – even if that participation simply entails bearing witness to the exotic testimonies of 'other' people's problems? In the Western understanding of democracy, everyone – in theory – has a right to be heard. However, in popular theatre – theatre made by the people, for the people – the audience should – again, in theory – be limited to members of the community who are affected by the issues at play. These contradictory views present a dilemma for LT practitioners to consider.

Both Augusto Boal (1998) and Jan Selman (2000) add to this discussion, though neither offers a finite solution. Boal, in his description of forum theatre, strictly cautions the joker against allowing an 'evangelist' intervention in which an audience member who has no experience with the oppression being depicted comes on stage to demonstrate or advise the protagonist how s/he should proceed. Likewise, if an audience member comes on stage and provides an unrealistic or seemingly 'magic' solution, it is the facilitator/joker's responsibility to interrupt the process and consult with the actors and audience members as to the feasibility of the intervention. The probability of either event occurring probably increases with the increase of perceived or real differences in social positioning between audience members and actors, as was potentially experienced in the move of the *Practicing Democracy* show from the East side of Vancouver to the West.

Selman (2000) also provides concrete examples of this dilemma when she describes her observations at popular theatre festivals in Canada. She writes:

> In my view the work that (unfortunately) suffered most when brought to festivals was the work created and performed by communities. These shows tended to suffer most in translation. When out of context, their theatrical and performance weaknesses suddenly mattered much more than when the who was performing resonated with the who that was watching and listening. (pp. 80–1)

Similarly, she speaks of a particular forum theatre piece that sparked controversy at a 1985 festival:

> The piece was a story about domestic violence and it was performed for a group of women survivors as well as miscellaneous festival participants . . . It raised, for me, huge ethical questions: when women who had lived with family violence set out to intervene, in front of many 'voyeurs' (by that I mean, those who had no experience with domestic violence and/or no relationship with the survivor group), and when those survivors, because of the forum formula, are caused to 'fail' in their interventions in the name of 'deepening the analysis', the fallout is highly problematic. (p. 81)

Clarifying the intent of the theatre and limiting or structuring the audience accordingly could potentially resolve these two issues.

In light of these dilemmas, the role of joker cannot be taken lightly. The ability to recognise evangelical and magic interventions, and to mediate effectively requires both sensitivity to the issues at hand and acute facilitation skills, as the potential exists to damage sometimes vulnerable performers. While previously unaware audience members may be moved to action in the near or distant future, the position of audience is in many ways a position of privilege. Audience members have the right to remain silent, to remain disengaged and dispassionate consumers of a theatrical experience: voyeurs. The actors – those whose lives are immediately affected by the issues – have no such luxury.

Inside the concept of 'voyeur' there are two complementary roles: the person being watched and the person experiencing some sense of pleasure by doing the watching. While LT in particular and forum theatre in general present possibilities for participants to feel violated by this voyeurism, it must also be acknowledged that there exists an equally powerful possibility for audience education and actor empowerment. Despite the complexities raised above, Diamond was unyielding in his belief that 'some very profound interventions and conversations happened on the West Side, EXACTLY because the play was an articulation of a world that the West Side (in general) is not familiar with' (personal communication, 19 January 2005, emphasis in original). Moreover, he argued that if one of the goals of this project was to practise democracy through public dialogue, 'why would we want to limit the audience or interveners? Doing so, I believe, only serves to keep communities polarised' (personal communication, 19 January 2005). This returns us to the idea that in ideal forms of democracy, everyone should have a right to participate. As such, a key insight of this research is that LT does not lead to either voyeurism or education and empowerment; the potential always exists for all three.

By portraying the reality of people living in poverty and affected by Provincial cutbacks to social services, the play was successful in raising awareness and promoting dialogue around these important issues with over 6,000 Vancouver residents. This was particularly true during the performances on the West side of Vancouver, as Diamond (2004) notes in his final report:

> When we got to the scenes with the food, the dumpster and the police, many of these people were shocked, terribly shocked to understand the depth of the problem. One person said from the seats that he was certain that if people really knew what the cuts to welfare meant, what the Provincial Government has done across the Province would be completely unacceptable. It's that people don't know, he said. "Why doesn't the media really deal with the issues the way this play is doing?"

Diamond goes on to add:

> Interestingly, in my own focus of trying to keep us in a realm of getting
> interventions that the City can do something about, I have lost sight,
> in a way, of the educating we are doing about the results of Provincial
> Government policy – especially this last week on the affluent West Side
> – in the Premier's riding, the Premier's Constituency. I am certain
> many of the people who have come to the show this last week would
> have voted for him in the last election. This project has been operating
> on many levels. (pp. 68–9)

Audience members I interviewed expressed a similar coming to awareness, in particular around the danger of staying in homeless shelters:

> She didn't want to go to the shelter . . . because she felt it was
> dehumanising and she felt she was being warehoused . . . From what I
> heard tonight it seems like an all-female [shelter] is needed, [a place
> where] they don't get into abusive situations. (Audience member A)

> I only vaguely knew about . . . how people felt abused at shelters
> and wouldn't go to them because of, well, because sometimes they've
> been kicked out and because they didn't feel safe. And it was interest-
> ing when [one actor] talked about how it's a business and that was
> hard to hear. I mean, to me it's a business of caring. (Audience
> member B)

Although both of these audience members worked in social service
fields, neither had first-hand experience in a homeless shelter and
consequently did not realise the extent of some individuals' reluctance
to use shelters. During the four performances I attended, I learned
equally important lessons around living in dumpsters, exchanging sex for
a safe place to sleep, strategies for stealing and hoarding food, police
brutality toward prostitutes, and other issues largely outside of
mainstream middle-class Canadian reality.

Finally, the empowering experience of individuals who participated
in the larger community workshop should be recognised. Although I did
not interview any participants as part of my study, Diamond speaks
repeatedly about the high level of enthusiasm and commitment made by

most participants in his projects. Referring to this project in particular, he states:

> In the closing circle, many talked about how unusual it is to be somewhere where they feel accepted, and where what they have to say is valued. They have said that they often are told this is going to be the case, but it turns out to be false.
>
> (Diamond, 2004b, p. 19)

While the structural barriers some of these participants face may potentially remain in place despite this creative attempt at generating new municipal policies, it is nevertheless important to acknowledge and value the skills gained, the connections made, and the positive experiences had by participants during the theatre workshop process.

Closing thoughts

In this chapter I have outlined Headlines Theatre's commitment to democracy and social justice through this legislative theatre project. I have confirmed that both the plays and the community workshops are valuable in and of themselves, as they serve to both stimulate dialogue, and raise awareness around local issues, as well as provide workshop participants with valuable work and training experiences. I have nevertheless described some of the challenges faced during the implementation phase of this experiment, despite the fact that it was an innovative opportunity for the public to have direct input into municipal policy creation. A key lesson for future projects is to solidify a mechanism for implementing new laws and policies to ensure that change occurs at a structural as well as an individual level. This may in turn override any potential for harm due to merely voyeuristic audience participation.

As the policy recommendations make their way through committees, task forces, and other bureaucratic hoops, we are reminded that public consultation, including the general public input during LT performances is only one step in a much longer process. Overall, this project is exemplary of the long and complicated road to social change; but, with organisations such as Headlines at the lead, diverse opportunities for democratic participation are continually being created, and with them comes the hope to keep on walking.

Acknowledgements

I would like to thank both David Diamond and the editors, Darlene Clover and Joyce Stalker, for their helpful comments on earlier drafts of this chapter. I would also like to acknowledge Marge Reitsma-Street for her support during the pilot stages of the research.

References

Ball, S. (1995) 'The influence of Boal on theatre in education in Britain', *Contemporary Theatre Review*, Vol. 3 No. 1, pp. 79–85.

Boal, A. (1979) *Theatre of the oppressed* (A. Charles and M.L. McBride, trans.). New York: Urizen Books.

Boal, A. (1998) *Legislative theatre* (A. Jackson, trans.). New York: Routledge.

Boal, A. (2002) *Games for actors and non-actors* (2nd ed., A. Jackson trans.). New York: Routledge.

Butterwick, S. (2002) 'Your story/my story/our story: Performing interpretation in participatory theatre', *The Alberta Journal of Educational Research*, Vol. 48, No. 3, pp. 240–53.

Butterwick, S. (2003) 'Re/searching speaking and listening across difference: Exploring feminist coalition politics through participatory theatre', *Qualitative Studies in Education*, Vol. 16, No. 3, pp. 449–65.

Byam, L. D. (1999) *Community in motion: Theatre for development in Africa.* Westport, CT: Bergin & Garvey.

City of Vancouver. (2004, September 15) Administrative report on City of Vancouver initiatives related to the recommendations in Practicing Democracy: A Legislative Theatre Project. (RTS No.: 04517; CC File

No.: 4657). Vancouver, BC. Retrieved January 10, 2005, from: http://www.headlinestheatre.com/pd/finalreports/CityHallreport.pdf

Diamond, D. (2004a) *A joker's guide to Theatre for Living* (rev. ed.). Vancouver, BC: Headlines Theatre.

Diamond, D. (2004b) *Practicing democracy: Final report.* Vancouver, BC: Headlines Theatre. Retrieved January 10, 2005 from: http://www. headlinestheatre.com/pd/finalreports/PDArtisticdirectorReport.pdf

Diamond, D. and Gallant, C. (2004, May 6) *Legislative theatre: Presentation to City Council.* Vancouver, BC: Headlines Theatre. Retrieved January 10, 2005 from: http://www.headlinestheatre.com/pd/finalreports/pdcity hallpresentation.pdf

Filewod, A. (1998) 'The Mummers Troupe, the Canada Council, and the production of theatre history', *Theatre Research in Canada,* Vol. 19, No. 1. Retrieved August 28 2004, from: http://www.lib.unb.ca/ Texts/TRIC/bin/getPrint.cgi?directory=vol19_1/filewod/&filename= filewod.html

Gallagher, K. (2001) *Drama education in the lives of girls: Imagining possibilities.* Toronto, ON: University of Toronto Press.

Gallant, C. (2004, April 21) *Practicing democracy: A legislative theatre project: Recommendations to Vancouver City Council.* Vancouver, BC: Gallant Solutions. Retrieved January 10, 2005 from: http://www.headlines theatre.com/pd/finalreports/PDlegislativereport.pdf

Gillespie, P. P. (1995) 'Feminist theory of theatre: Revolution or revival?' In K. Laughlin & C. Schuler (eds.), *Theatre and feminist aesthetics* (pp. 100–30). Mississauga, ON: Associated University Presses.

Headlines Theatre website. (2005) Vancouver, BC. http://www.headlines theatre.com/

Hinsdale, M. A., Lewis, H. and Waller, S. M. (1995) *It comes from the people: Community development and local theology.* Philadelphia: Temple Press.

Legarda, M. (2002) In D. Adams and A. Goldbard (eds), *Community, culture and globalization* (pp. 335–52). New York: The Rockefeller Foundation.

Manyozo, L. (2002) 'Community theatre without community partici-pation? Reflections on development support communication pro-grammes in Malawi', *Convergence*, Vol. 3,5 No. 4, pp. 55–70.

Mda, Z. (1993) *When people play people*. London: Zed Books.

Nelson, J. (1993) 'Improvisational theatre helps teen mothers raise sights' [Electronic version], *Children Today*, Vol. 22, No. 2, pp. 24–7.

Obeyesekere, R. (1999) *Sri Lankan theatre in a time of terror: Political satire in a permitted space*. Thousand Oaks, CA: Sage.

Plastow, J. and Tsehaye, S. (1998) 'Making theatre for a change: Two plays of the Eritrean liberation struggle'. In R. Boon and J. Plastow (eds), *Theatre for a change: Performance and culture on the world stage* (pp. 55–75). New York: Cambridge University Press.

Practicing Democracy website. (2005) Vancouver, BC: Headlines Theatre. http://www.headlinestheatre.com/pd/finalreports/index.html

Prentki, T. and Selman, J. (2000) *Popular theatre and political culture: Britain and Canada in focus*. Portland, OR: Intellect.

Selman, J. (2000) 'The development of popular theatre in Canada'. In T. Prentki and J. Selman, *Popular theatre in political culture: Britain and Canada in focus* (pp. 73–84). Portland, OR: Intellect Books.

Steward, D. (1970) *Stage left*. Dover, DE: The Tanager Press.

CHAPTER 6

Journey to a (bi)cultural identity

Fabric art/craft and social justice
in Aotearoa New Zealand

Nora West and Joyce Stalker

Introduction

Edward Said (1993) suggested that imperialism was the practice and theory of a dominant metropolitan centre ruling over a distant territory. The old British Empire was once such a centre and it taught many New Zealanders to see themselves through British eyes as exiles from and marginal to the real world. Although we have had a long journey towards political self-determination and a cultural identity that no longer sees England as Home, we continue to struggle to create a unique identity and to acknowledge a bicultural heritage based in the Treaty of Waitangi.

Within this context, fabric art/craft has played many important roles. This chapter explores connections among protest activities, the fabric art/craft world and the development of Aotearoa (Land of the long white cloud) New Zealand's cultural identity over the last 25 years. It focuses on the role of fabric as medium, signifier and a site for art, activist messages and social learning. It reveals the work of our fabric artists as educators who have helped to reflect and shape our cultural identities.

The chapter begins by presenting the Aotearoa New Zealand context which shapes our cultural identity and influences the nature of our fabric crafts. It then gives a brief overview of the nature of fabric art/craft in Aotearoa New Zealand followed by a discussion of the roles of fabric artists. These roles are illustrated by examples of fabric art/craft as a site for explicit protest, cultural democracy and emergent cultural identity. The chapter ends with a brief summary and comment on the potential of fabric art/craft.

The Aotearoa New Zealand context

In order to understand the particular context of this inquiry we need to remember that Aotearoa New Zealand is a country more remote from its nearest neighbours than any other landmass on the globe. These islands broke away from Gondwanaland at the evolutionary stage of the reptile, making the ancient tuatara lizard the one animal that did not arrive here by air or sea. It is thus a land peopled by immigrants – seen differently by each new wave of arrivals – and very sparsely peopled, to be sure. In a land the size of Great Britain, there are just over four million souls.

The first human voyagers came to this isolated land 1,000 years ago, voyaging south from east Polynesia. The first inhabitants of Aotearoa New Zealand relied on wood, stone and flax for domestic and spiritual artefacts. The first European settlers studied their Maori culture – and that of the subsequent voyagers – with a detached and anthropological interest. They ranked Maori's taonga (spiritual artefact) as savage, 'other' and inferior up to the first half of the twentieth century. This attitude slowly evolved in the second half of the century to an appreciation of indigenous culture as a valuable component of Aotearoa New Zealand's independent bicultural identity.

In the last 25 years, immigrants from the Pacific Islands under Aotearoa New Zealand's protection have introduced a third distinct strand of immigrants and more recently still there has been an influx of Asian peoples. These co-exist, not always easily, with new European settlers and returning expatriates, to produce a cosmopolitan and culturally-diverse population.

The cultural identity of Aotearoa New Zealand has thus been problematic ever since the arrival of the colonising Europeans in the last century united most Maori tribes into a common front. The newcomers were tau iw (Others) to the indigenous population, who were variously seen as noble savages or inferior natives by the European settlers. Out-numbered by Maori, the British colonisers signed the Treaty of Waitangi, in 1890, to ensure a partnership relationship between Maori and Pakeha (European/white).

With each wave of new immigrants, this already unstable mix struggles to blend into a nation while retaining distinct identities for its various cultural communities. Notions of social justice for the first settlers involved priority rights. Recent immigrants, often refugees from harsh conditions, tend to believe in 'fair shares all around'. The customs, practices, languages, values and worldviews that define us as a nation are constantly contested. As the Ministry of Social Development (2003, para. 2) noted: 'Most New Zealanders acknowledge that they live in a multicultural society, yet also acknowledge that maori culture has a unique place . . . People may identify themselves as New Zealanders in some circumstances and as part of a particular culture – maori, Chinese or Scottish, for example – in other circumstances . . . maori culture may form one aspect of national identity, since it is unique to New Zealand and forms part of our identity in the outside world.'

We have also been affected by global and local political shifts over a quarter century of significant collapses and realignments of boundaries worldwide. In the last 25 years, this country has begun to perceive itself independently (Wolff, 1993). This is due to a number of historical shifts in allegiance, some from without, and some from within. The founding of the European Economic Community, for example, moved Britain's allegiance away from its Commonwealth ties. This has had serious repercussions in the loss of traditional markets for our farmers. It has also meant that after 150 years we are shaking off our traditional loyalties and our status as a docile colony of the British Empire. The process of decolonisation is implicit in much of our changing sense of political and cultural identity. We are no longer a far-flung outpost of the British Empire. We have established our country as an independent political democracy. The journey towards cultural democracy is a more recent story. It is linked to our 'third way' government which encourages wide participation in the arts, in the belief that it is a cornerstone of a just and equitable society (Creative New Zealand, 2006).

At home, the government is re-examining the Treaty of Waitangi and has set up a tribunal to redress Maori grievances over land confiscations by nineteenth century British settlers. A new generation of activists has arisen. Grassroots opposition to the threat of nuclear warfare has challenged the ANZUS pact between Australia, Aotearoa New Zealand and the United States. Groups opposed sporting Common-wealth ties with South Africa in a series of dramatic confrontations that marked the 1981/1982 Springbok rugby tour. The most recent focus for activist energies has been on environmental issues such as multinational operations in native forest logging, and genetically-engineered crop trials. In 1999, in accordance with these views, voters elected Green politicians into positions of government influence (Beatson, 1994) through a Mixed Member Proportional voting system.

Our decolonisation is not complete, however, for at the same time that we loosen our ties to Britain, we still defer in artistic matters to Australia, the USA and Europe. Said (1993) identifies this condition as cultural imperialism. It appears that we too readily accept, rather than adapt, the values of other cultures.

In sum, key elements which define our context and shape our cultural identity, or perhaps more accurately, our (bi)cultural identity, include the Maori culture, multiculturalism, decolonisation and cultural imperialism. Below, we explore the ways in which our fabric crafts reflect these phenomena.

A brief overview of fabric art/crafts in Aotearoa New Zealand

Given the context above, where do fabric crafts feature? As a long-time fabric artist in Aotearoa New Zealand, Nora has noticed fabrics' prevalence and power in the fields of both art and activism. Fabric art/craft can effectively reveal and reinforce the country's complex identities. Those who produce them are, at heart, adult educators, for they teach us about our culture and help us learn about its limitations and possibilities. Fabric art/craft provides us with effective sites for non-violent protest. This role is facilitated by fabric's symbolic marginality and by its logistical/technical characteristics.

In the first instance, fabric is a symbol for the marginalised, the Other, the Outsider. There is an ironic symmetry between fabric art/craft and the geographical location of Aotearoa New Zealand. Both carry a message of marginalisation. In fabric crafts this marginalisation exists both in relation to the fine arts and in its use as a medium of marginalised groups.

As an artist, fabric has been central to Nora's practice and she has observed first-hand that fabric crafts are marginalised in relation to the fine arts. For many years the art world has relegated them to the realm of craft and the domestic (Parker, 1983) and a secondary status. Any discussion of fibre practice inevitably invokes this age-old art/craft debate. Despite challenges made to fine art criteria or practice through-out this century, the perception remains that the technical aspects of the construction and decoration of applied arts are inferior to the techniques of painting, printmaking and sculpture (Schamroth, 1998). This perception ignores the fact that printmaking on paper and textiles requires very similar technical skills, while the design of quilts and woven rugs calls for the same subtle sense of colour and shape as that required for a painting or sculpture. The prejudiced nature of this view has more to do with fabric's association with women's crafts than with any rational argument. In other words, fabric's close association with the feminine condemns it to be perceived of less value in a patriarchal culture (Stalker, 2003, 2005; Parker, 1983).

Aotearoa New Zealand gives us two interesting insights into fabric crafts' marginality. First, as a leisure activity, fabric crafts are not only marginalised in relation to fine arts, but they are marginalised in relation to male-dominated sports. Although this may be true of many countries, in this country, male sports are almost revered. An 'important' All Black's rugby game can virtually stop the nation and the 'first 15' players are national heroes. Within this context, fabric art/craft is highly feminised and attracts very little attention or respect. We can only hope that fabric's re-appearance in Aotearoa New Zealand as a medium within conceptual art practice indicates a slackening in the power of these patriarchal values. Second, it is a strange anomaly that, while Maori raranga whaikairo (flax weaving) has gained acceptance as an integral part of Maori art, fibre work of equal skill by European women remains undervalued by comparison. This incongruence parallels the complex cultural tensions discussed above. In both instances, however, it is possible to be hopeful, for it is precisely because its identity is unstable and unfixed, that fabric work is hard to categorise and thus can play a role in fostering social justice.

Fabric's marginality is dependent on more than its relationship to the fine arts. It is also marginal because its marginalisation converges with the marginality of the key artists who use fabric: women, ethnic, immigrant and gay groups (Rowley, 1997). In other words, fabric is often a medium of the oppressed and disempowered, practised in old folks' homes and mental hospitals, in prisons and refugee camps, in the drawing rooms of wealthy women fearful of expressing their own opinions. It is this marginality that makes fabric the ideal medium for messages of creative resistance to social injustice. For an artist to choose the fabric medium is to state an intrinsically political message. For an activist to use fabric in protest banners or street theatre is to employ non-violent, creative strategies that, in Aotearoa New Zealand, seem to be not only more ethically appropriate, but often more politically persuasive than violent guerrilla action.

Above, we have explored the effectiveness of fabric art/craft for non-violent protest in terms of its marginality in relation to the fine arts and in its use as a medium of marginalised groups. There is another aspect of fabric which facilitates its role as a powerful site for non-violent protest: its logistical and technical characteristics. The skills and processes of working with them constitute a universal language through which it is possible to transmit and sometimes challenge the traditional values of specific cultures, generally through female domestic channels. Since those skills and processes can be learned, transmitted and used by both the literate and illiterate, they undermine hierarchies and transcend cultural boundaries. They have a special potential to draw together the global diaspora of women and the oppressed.

The intrinsic properties of fabric contribute to this language. Fabric is generally cheap, soft, absorbent, portable and thus particularly suited to subversive political actions. The softness of fabric means its shape is unfixed, protean. This makes it easily portable and concealable. The Aotearoa New Zealand documentary *Punitive damage*, by Annie Goldson (1999) includes footage of protestors in East Timor defying demonstration bans by concealing their homemade banners under their T-shirts until the signal came to hold them up in an instantaneous display. Similarly, banners can be hung, illicitly, just long enough to be captured on film and transmitted round the world.

Fabric is absorbent, mopping up blood, sweat, tears and all those other body fluids that the ruling order wishes would disappear. It folds and furls, covers and clothes, wraps and bandages, hides and heals. It is intimately associated with the body. Indeed in its use as a bandage, shroud, veil, dress, disguise, fabric functions as an extension of the body, mediating between our vulnerable flesh and the world.

Finally, fabric is resilient and can be recycled many times. Early colonial pioneering women saved every last scrap of worn-out clothing for their quilts and rag rugs. Even in the throwaway society of contemporary Aotearoa New Zealand, garments often cover several bodies before, via op shop and clothing bins, they are recycled into paper and workshop rags. Its connections, therefore, are with the body rather than the intellect, and with the workers rather than the rulers of the body politic. These are inherently political and resistant alliances.

In sum, fabric art/craft in Aotearoa New Zealand, as in many other countries, can be an effective site for non-violent protest precisely because of its symbolic marginality and logistical/technical characteristics. However, fabric art/craft in Aotearoa New Zealand holds a special relationship to those characteristics. It is Other and marginal within a marginal context, yet it resonates, perhaps in a colonised way, with the marginalisation of fabric art/craft around the world. Similarly, the subtle, subversive characteristics of fabric art/craft mirror fabric crafts elsewhere, yet they hold a special role within a country in which cultural identity and tensions remain problematic and sensitive. Below, we explore those ideas as they were expressed in specific fabric art/craft projects.

The role of fabric artists in Aotearoa New Zealand

The focus of this paper is on the role of fabric artists in Aotearoa New Zealand to facilitate the journey to our (bi)cultural identity. It is unlikely that many of the artists detailed below would identify themselves as adult educators. Yet that is what they are, for they are key players on a deeply educational journey toward our (bi)cultural identity and by implication, social justice. Cultural identity formation is a complex, dynamic process but basically it allows us to set ourselves apart and distinguish ourselves as unique from other cultures and societies. What is important here is that it can, to some extent, be taught and learned.

On the one hand, fabric artists can help us learn about, preserve and support the dominant culture and indeed, colonise other cultures (Hood, 2001; Moore, 1994). On the other hand, fortunately, fabric artists also can have a more positive learning agenda, for they can reveal issues related to Maori culture, multiculturalism, decolonisation and cultural imperialism. They can help us to identify, deconstruct and un-learn our prejudices, biases and assumptions. They can help us, as a nation, to create a (bi)cultural identity more sensitive to social justices and injustices. In this respect, the artists discussed below are activist adult educators. Some attempt to reveal oppressions, complexities, and historical disadvantages. Others hint at the unique strengths which arise from our heritage and which can lead us into a better future. All of them ask us to reflect and act to create a better nation. Below, we explore these ideas as illustrated by fabric art/craft's sites of explicit protest, cultural democracy and emergent cultural identity.

Fabric art/craft as a site of explicit protest

In Aotearoa New Zealand, protest banners have been explicit sites of political protest and resistance by marginalised groups, for many years. Our early protest banners were influenced by those of the great Trades Unions in England in Victorian times (Union Trades & Labour Council of South Australia Arts Program, 1987); they reflected the unions' power and wealth in their magnificently ornate, commercially manufactured productions. They were grand examples of the synergy which can happen between art and politics. Yet some would argue that we should 'keep art out of politics'. It seems to us that when someone says that, the underlying meaning is 'Don't rock the boat'. Political change, for most people, means unwelcome upheaval. However established, whatever the injustice or waste or sheer boredom of any system, most of us prefer to learn the rules and live by them or go around them, rather than embark on a radical overhaul. But politics is the science and art of government; and government is about maintaining the status quo as much as it is about change. Those in power (not just those elected, but all their powerful supporters) work to maintain or shift our attitudes in accordance with their own tastes and values. Thus every aspect of our culture is either endorsed or suppressed by ideological means (Foster, 1983). Fabric art/craft is a powerful tool in this struggle.

By the 1990s in Aotearoa New Zealand, as elsewhere, union power was in decline, but today marches still take place on May Day to commemorate International Workers' Day. Banners play a key role in them. Contemporary fabric art/craft worker Malcolm Harrison continues to use banners to make his social justice statements (see http://www.textiles.org.nz/profiles/malcolmh/). He trained as a tailor, but has been internationally acclaimed over the last 30 years for work that joins virtuoso fabric skills to a brilliant design sensibility. He made his May Day Banner in the 1990s to acknowledge his father's union membership. It employs the large format traditional scale; but the design is exuberantly contemporary. Combining the aesthetics of Pacific Island quilts and street graffiti, it is a flag for a new generation to rally to, made with a devotional craftsmanship that reinforces and transcends its message.

Harrison continues a proud tradition, for in Aotearoa New Zealand, Women's Suffragists, environmental and nuclear-free lobby groups and indigenous rights activists all have employed fabric processes and materials to articulate their grievances. Often the means of production is amateur and domestic. None the less, many a women's group in the 1980s, like WILPF, (Women's International League for Peace and Freedom) used them as a place to learn and teach about women's rights. They raised their consciousness while composing slogans, designing images and sewing them onto donated fabric. In a reversal of the swords into ploughshares adage, they turned bed sheets into battle flags.

Large multinational activist organisations also use banners and often employ commercial billboard technology to parody and undermine the messages of corporate culture. These organisations operate inside Aotearoa New Zealand and again exemplify how our citizens have simultaneously learned to accept outside ideas and yet identify as an independent nation with a voice of protest.

Greenpeace's involvement with Aotearoa New Zealand serves as a good example of this complex, learned identity. In the late 1990s, when huge PVC banners promoting the internationally renowned musical *Les Miserables!* were hung from the sides of Auckland's Aotea Centre, they were temporarily joined by Greenpeace counterfeits, nimbly installed by abseiling activists. Pictures of the new banner, Les Miserables Bastards! were widely disseminated through the media to a large audience appreciative of their message of protest against French nuclear testing in the Pacific. This was a particularly popular stand among New Zealanders because in 1980, the French sank the *Rainbow Warrior* in Auckland harbour just before it was to leave to protest nuclear tests at the south Pacific island of Mururoa (Eyley, 1997). New Zealanders' co-operation with Greenpeace in the banner protest demonstrates its identity. Aotearoa New Zealand and Mururoa both share a position which is marginal to the dominant political power, largely invisible to most of the world and thus a 'safe' place to test one's nuclear bombs.

In brief, the history of protest actions of the last 25 years reads as a continuous narrative of de-colonisation. The present generation of Aotearoa New Zealand artists/activists share some of the same beliefs in social justice that inspired early Quaker settlers, and perhaps the original Polynesian voyagers. Yet, New Zealanders are constantly learning a new identity which separates us from the English and global colonisers and accommodates our ever changing mix of cultures.

Fabric art/craft as a site for cultural democracy

The second illustration of the ways in which fabrics resist the dominant culture is more subtle than that above. It is a gentle, persuasive process in which art is made more accessible, more democratised. While fine arts are created for a narrow audience which shares a specialised language, crafts usually are accessible to, and inclusive of, a broader spectrum of society. While Aotearoa New Zealand prides itself on its political democracy, some would argue that culturally, it remains autocratic, with certain art forms and styles favoured by a powerful cabal. A theory of cultural democracy is thus a useful concept in this chapter, for it argues that all individuals are capable of original expression and have a unique contribution to make.

Similarly, notions of originality and uniqueness are learned deeply by New Zealanders. Cultural democracy suggests that societies flourish when they foster wide participation in the arts, and that the value of an artwork, the product of the creative construction and learning process, lies in its effectiveness, that is, how appropriate it is for its site, public and function (Braden, 1978; Laughton, 1993). In this view the value of the craft/artwork is not exclusively aesthetic, but includes therapeutic and often more importantly, social functions. This is a holistic view, based on the politics of inclusion; on how to live well as much as how to be a good artist; it is a view that locates art making in a social context, claiming that our responsibilities as people underpin our privileges as artists.

On this reading fabric art/craft scores highly as a language accessible to a wide and diverse audience. It is a place where voice can be both learned and practised. Fabric art/craft refers broadly to that area of cultural production that combines textile materials and techniques into products of innovative design and/or handcrafted construction. When people bring any creative artefact into existence they are being active producers and transmitters rather than passive consumers of culture. This voicing of identity is transformative; it produces a sense of self-worth and also of the cultural value of the product. It is more than therapeutic because it reaches others; it is a tool of communication, a language; and thus a politicising act.

In Aotearoa New Zealand, the notion of cultural democracy meshes nicely with its self-image as a social democracy. It is also enhanced by the current Labour-coalition government's support of the arts and culture through educational programmes, scholarships and financial assistance to artists which is similar to the unemployment benefit. Below are several examples which illustrate the ways in which New Zealanders have reflected and fostered cultural democracy through fabric craft.

The AIDS Memorial Quilt

The first and best-known example of fabric art/craft as a site of cultural democracy in Aotearoa New Zealand is probably its AIDS Memorial Quilt. As Marshall McLuhan (1989) so famously remarked 'The medium is the message' – and never louder or clearer than in this quilt. This project breaks two key silences. On the one hand, as a public display of low-status fabric craft, the quilt is effectively a political act of resistance in and of itself. It breaks fabric craft's silence, gives it a voice and insists on visibility. On the other hand, the quilt form is particularly clever in that it often resists the dominant, masculine culture of the individual artefact created by a solo artist. The quilt's role as comforter has made it a favourite site for collaborative statements. It began as the gays' political statement about the public and government's dismissal of the AIDS epidemic, evolved into a famous therapeutic process/event and as a result of the involvement of thousands of grieving people, re-emerged as a strong, collective political statement about the public and government's dismissal of the AIDS epidemic.

Anslie Yardley, who documented the Aotearoa New Zealand project in her Master's thesis, links the project to:

the emergence of feminist art in the 70s and the significance of fabric art/craft as a political statement in that movement . . . It is not an accident, in the case of the Quilt, that this form of expression was chosen as a symbol of love and remembrance and as a means of making a strong political statement (1994, p. 71)

The Aotearoa New Zealand project was officially launched on World AIDS Day 1988, is constantly growing, and moves among various sites to raise awareness and create positive changes in attitudes and behaviour (Yardley, 1994). It was based on the Australian AIDS Memorial Quilt Project which was the first, and remains the largest of the 27 international projects to result from the United States-based *Names Project*. This fabric relationship across the Tasman Sea reflects our on-going affiliation with our neighbour. As our colonial ties fade, the down-under relationship is sustained, dependent partly on a shared understanding of geographic marginality, shared workforces and sport. It might also reflect our acceptance of cultural deference even as we create exemplars of cultural democracy.

Cook Island Tivaevae
A second example of fabric crafts' role of fostering cultural democracy is evident in the cultural evolution of the Cook Island tivaevae (Rongokea, 2001). These appliqué bedspreads evolved as a fabric art/craft form in the late nineteenth century; a wonderful hybrid born of the sewing skills taught by British missionary wives to Cook Island women who applied their own exuberant colour and design sense to the production of two metre square, communally sewn bedspreads. They have a high ceremonial value in wedding and funeral use in the islands, but were until recently considered only of anthropological interest. They have recently achieved art status in Aotearoa New Zealand through a number of shows in public art galleries. One of the first was in Dunedin, in 1998, entitled *Tiare Taina o te Kuki Airani – Tivaevae from Cook Island women of Dunedin.* The large and intricate works were hung on the wall like paintings, and in that context their breathtaking rhythms and singing colours proved equal in power to any painting exhibition. Some of the works were presented in progress, and the presence of the women sewing melted the gallery chill. This bringing into the gallery space of outsider artefacts has raised the value of the works, brought in a larger

audience, and contributed to mutual respect between two diverse cultures. In other words, they were exceptionally effective locations of learning and teaching for social justice.

World Court Quilt

The third example, The World Court Quilt (see West, 2000) was a similar project. It was co-ordinated and largely sewn by Joanne Bains, in 1994. She has made a life project of sewing quilts for peace, women and the environment. Its purpose is to persuade high-level international politicians that the Pacific should be independent and nuclear free. Each block is made by a different school or community group, using techniques of appliqué and reverse appliqué, batik, screen print and hand embroidery. Many are inspired by Cook Island tivaevae. These designs have become iconic in Aotearoa New Zealand culture and represent the diversity of the country. Others depict local flora and fauna, all designs appropriate for messages of resistance to the cultural imperialism implicit in Pacific nuclear testing, while the quilt's role as comforter opposes the destructive function of nuclear bombs. The quilt made the journey to the World Court in The Hague with an Aotearoa New Zealand delegation, and is now at Te Papa, the National Museum in Wellington.

Fabrics in prison

The final example of the cultural democracy embedded in fabric crafts/arts focuses on prison fabric craft/art. While all rehabilitive programmes have a social justice component, recreational art has a unique role to play in the lives of people largely deprived of creative opportunities. The transformative power of fabric, in particular, is evident in fabric painting programmes run in long-term men's prisons. Whereas woodcarving requires sharp tools, that may be used as weapons, silk painting needs little room or equipment. Traditional Maori rafter patterns translate well into fabric, with enchanting results. The lightness of the silk and the brightness of the colours transform the designs, and the inherent qualities of silk – its softness, translucence, colour absorbency – make for a harmonious and therapeutic learning experience. In women's prisons, flax weaving and quilt making teach skills that enhance self-esteem, while providing a setting which resembles a study circle for relaxed discussions and reflection on personal issues. There is an additional bonus in terms of fabric art as a consumable, with opportunities for small-scale production of silk scarves and ties.

The four examples above demonstrate the ways in which fabric crafts can foster cultural democracy. They also illustrate the ways in which cultural democracy and adult education converge. Fabric crafts act as bandages of the body politic as they bind together people of diverse cultural and social groups with the familiar artefacts of domestic life. They allow each person their own particular cultural expression yet, with a common language of fabric, fibre and embellishment they accommodate a diverse range of groups. Often collaborative, fabric art/craft can be a consciousness-raising activity which furthers reflections on both the negative and positive aspects of our (bi)cultural identities. As well, fabric crafts can be created outside the market from free scraps, and in this way, subvert the dominant consumerist discourse. In total, the cultural democracy role of fabric art/craft shares many characteristics with activist adult education and its commitment to social justice.

Fabric as a site of emergent cultural identity

As Aotearoa New Zealand faces the 21st century, it is struggling to balance its bicultural and multicultural identities. Legally bound to a bicultural Treaty agreement, we have an obligation to retain a partnership between Maori and Pakeha. Yet New Zealanders cannot ignore the changing face of the country. Increasingly we are a diverse nation composed of Pacific peoples, Asians, South Africans, Somalians and peoples from around the world. The use of fabric media in works destined for an art world audience often deliberately deploys fabric as a signifier. Flax and fibre have long been staples of the Aotearoa New Zealand economy, skilfully fashioned by women, both indigenous Maori and settler Pakeha, into essential domestic artefacts. These associations add significance to the corporeal message of the fabric medium. Humble fabric is the stuff of survival and well equipped to bind the split in our consciousness, to reintegrate our politics into our culture. Below, we explore the work of two craft artists who are using fabric to explore our emerging (bi)cultural identity.

The first craft/art worker, Maureen Lander, negotiates the territory between Pakeha and Maori cultural practices by working within the terms and references of European fine art, while consistently using the traditional (Maori/women/craft) processes and materials of raranga

138

whaikairo (Maori pleating patterns). Lander lectures in material culture in the degree programme at Manukau Polytechnic's School of Arts and exhibits widely as a performance/installation artist. The exhibit, *This is not a kete* (basket), consists of a group of baskets, made by Lander, and scattered on the gallery floor. One of them is backlit, and elevated to a plinth, which is inscribed with the title words. The work conforms to the conventions of Eurocentric art discourse in referring to the work of Magritte, a famous surreal Belgian artist. She responds to his *This is not a pipe*, in order to question the art/craft role of kete weaving, and of the kete itself, within Aotearoa New Zealand gallery culture. Indeed, she says that this was the first time she perceived the kete, of which she had made hundreds, as a thing in itself, rather than a container for something else. She uses the humble connotations of flax and inserts them into high culture, disrupting the orthodox discourse and empowering and giving a new voice to those who use these traditional materials.

She gathered flax at all the places she stopped on the drive down to Wellington, and made 34 kete for the gallery presentation before the opening event. Lander's consistent engagement with traditional fibre techniques and processes rests on a strong theoretical base. Her works' acceptance within this country's fine art canon is evidenced by its exhibition in municipal art galleries.

The second fabric worker, Tame Iti, crosses over the boundaries of art, fabric and politics. He is the author of an unstable hybrid, one that resists definition as a fabric piece, a protest banner or an artwork. Tama Iti is a radical Maori activist of Ngai Tuhoe descent, for whom the boundaries of art and politics are meaningless. All his actions are instrumental to his major project, the re-empowerment of the Maori people. The work for which he is best known in the Aotearoa New Zealand art world is the inscribed horse blanket which he flung at Treaty negotiations Minister Doug Graham in the course of negotiations on behalf of his Tuhoe people.

Iti chose a deliberately stained blanket, taken off the back of a horse in the paddock, as the writing material for his tribal grievances, and Graham accepted it as a taonga (treasure), and had it placed under glass in his office at Parliament. Thereupon Iti sent him a bill for $10,000. The bill was never paid, but the blanket next appeared in the inaugural exhibition at the Adam Art Gallery, Victoria University, Wellington. Ten works from the collection were selected by 11 curators, who contextualised them with contemporary works. In this fine art setting, the significance of the blanket leaps forward, redolent of nineteenth century Pakeha/Maori trading, cover-ups, smothering, putting out fires. It speaks of poverty, injustice and defiance and it twists the heart.

These two works teach us about our historical identity and the need to create a new one which is more sensitive to our bicultural society. The flaxroots (our version of grassroots) nature of Lander's work grounds us quite literally in the abuses of Maori by Pakeha while Iti's blanket creates a visual challenge to political systems and our (bi)cultural identity. Both elevate the notions of Treaty obligations and biculturalism above that of multiculturalism. Their strong stances strike to the heart of the discourse which considers bicultural-multicultural tensions. Their work is a metaphor, a teaching tool, in which we learn, about the primacy of partnerships, the legitimacy of alternative craft forms and our politics. They challenge the Pakeha notion of art and intrude into spaces formerly dominated by Pakeha. They dare us to value Maoritanga (Maori culture/way of life) equally with Pakeha culture. In a globalised world, they bring us back to a key element of who we are as a nation. One could argue that these fabric artists are consummate adult educators.

Conclusion

This chapter has explored, through fabric craft, Aotearoa New Zealanders' journey toward a cultural-bicultural identity over the last twenty-five years. Its process of decolonisation and cultural imperialism when combined with an increasingly multicultural population and a legally-binding Treaty between Maori and Pakeha creates a unique context for fabric workers. These different threads of our identity are woven into our fabric art and crafts. We use them to make explicit protests, as tools to foster cultural democracy and to enhance our emerging (bi)cultural identity.

Despite the trivialisation of fabric art/craft in Aotearoa New Zealand, despite its bad image of kitsch tea cosies or mindless busywork, our fabric work is a strong tool for education and teaching the politics of who we are and who we might become. Fortunately in our small country, the 'fatal splitting of the aesthetic and political realms' (Said,

1995, p. unknown) has perhaps been less pronounced than elsewhere. Some of us have used effectively fabric's innate properties that make it an appropriate medium for subversive (bi)cultural statements. Our fabric art/craft has been inventive, impassioned, ingeniously wrought and articulate.

We do not need to think of ourselves as a far-flung outpost with little to offer in the area of fabric crafts made to further social justice. We have shown that we have the potential to use them as educational tools which can create cutting-edge strategies for a healthy, creative, ethical and equitable nation. Whether in the form of banners that push for reform of injustices, or artworks in galleries that confer respect on 'grandmothers' skills', making fabric art/craft is a therapeutic process, a bandaging of the wounds of the body politic incurred on the journey to our nationhood and a strong (bi)cultural identity.

References

Barnett S. and Wolf, R. (1989) *Aotearoa New Zealand! Aotearoa New Zealand!* London: Hodder and Stoughton.

Batra, E. (ed) (2003) *Crafting gender. Women and folk art in Latin America and the Caribbean.* London: Duke University Press.

Beatson, P. and Beatson, D. (eds) (1994) *The arts in Aotearoa* New Zealand: Themes and issues. Palmerston North: Massey University.

Braden, S. (1978) *Artists and people.* NY: Routledge and Keagan Paul.

Creative New Zealand (2006) *The arts in New Zealand.* Wellington, NZ: Creative New Zealand.

Eyley, C. (1997) *Protest at Muroroa: First hand accounts from the Aotearoa New Zealand-based flotilla.* Auckland: Tandem Press.

Foster, H. (ed) (1983) *The anti-aesthetic: Essays on post-modern culture.* CA: New Press.

Goldson, A. (1999) *Punitive damage* (Documentary movie). Auckland: First Run/Icarus Films.

Hood, Y. (2001) 'The culture of resistance: African American art quilts and self-defining', *Uncoverings*, Vol. 22, No. 14, p. 169.

Laughton, J. (1993) 'Cultural democracy, issues of multiculturalism, and the arts', *Journal of Arts Management, Law & Society*, Vol. 23, No. 2, Retrieved July 2006 from http://web.ebscohost.com.ezproxy. waikato.ac.nz

McLuhan, M. (1989) *The medium and the messenger.* Toronto: Random House.

Ministry of Social Development (2003) *The Social Report 2003.* Retrieved November 1, 2006, from http://www.socialreport.msd. govt.nz/2003

Parker, R. (1983) *The subversive stitch.* London: Women's Press.

Rongokea, L. (2001) *The art of tivaevae.* Auckland: Godwit.

Rowley, S. (1997) 'Introduction'. In S. Rowley (ed), *Craft and contemporary theory* (pp. xiv–xxvi). St. Leonards, NSW: Allen and Unwin.

Said, E. (1993) *Culture and imperialism.* London: Chatto and Windus.

Schamroth, H. (1998) *100 Aotearoa New Zealand craft artists.* Auckland, NZ: Random House.

Stalker, J. (2003) ' "Ladies' work" and feminist critical pedagogy'. In D. Flowers (ed) *Proceedings of the 44th Adult Education Research Conference* (pp. 399–404). San Francisco: SF State University.

Stalker, J. (2005) 'Fabricating new directions for women's learning: Case studies in fabric crafts and fashion'. In P. Jarvis (ed), *Human learning: An holistic approach* (pp. 168–82). London: Routledge.

Union Trades & Labour Council of South Australia Arts Program (1987) *Modern Trade Union Banners.* South Australia: Newstyle Printing.

West, N. (2000) *Fibre active.* Unpublished Master thesis. Auckland: Auckland University of Technology.

Wolff, J. (1993) *The social production of art*. UK: Palgrave Macmillan Publishers.

Yardley, A. (1994) *Unfolding: The story of the Australian and Aotearoa New Zealand AIDs quilt projects*. Harmondsworth, UK: Penguin Books.

Section Four

Art and community development

CHAPTER 7

Passion and politics through song

Recalling music to the arts-based debates in adult education

Francesca Albergato-Muterspaw and Tara Fenwick

Introduction

In arts–based approaches to educational research and practice, music does not yet tend to receive the emphasis accorded to expressive arts such as popular theatre. In fact, musical expression and participation itself, outside the creative act of composition, might easily be misunderstood as a technical process of reproduction with little inherent possibility for learning, inquiry and political activism.

Yet some adult educators have come to recognise and even promote music as a valid way of knowing (Kaltoft, 1999; Shaw & Martin, 2005), and music has been used for decades to enhance learning in formal, informal and non-formal settings (Bell, 2004). Many educators acknowledge the powerful role of song in social justice histories, such as the Canadian labour and African-American civil rights movements. Internationally and historically, song has established for itself a core role in building solidarity, shaping rhythms for collective activity, mobilising social resistance, and actually energising activist movements. This is in addition to the unique processes of sharing cultural, political and social information that occurs through participation in music. Singing is in fact one of the more inclusive forms of musical participation, requiring no special equipment, environment, or able-ness (deaf choirs are common). It is holistic in practice, uniting breath, vibration, language and synchronous connection with others.

In this chapter we outline the contribution of music to cultural animation and learning connected to social justice, with a focus on song and processes of singing. We draw on both music-learning literature and our respective experiences facilitating vocal groups and studying song: Francesca is a musicologist, vocalist and vocal conductor, and Tara began her working life as a community choir conductor. Couched in a critical context, we explore how music is a way of knowing; the physiological and emotional dimensions of song and singing and their relation to learning; the different communicative styles of music; and the relational dynamics of group musical participation, called 'ensemble'. Then we link these to social justice, examining the relation of music and particularly community choirs to activism and solidarity learning. We conclude with recommendations for educators interested in exploring musical expression and participation with learners.

Music as a way of knowing

The discussion surrounding music as a way of knowing is lengthy and complex. Dimensions range from specific consideration of cultural and social influences (gender, race, ethnicity, religion, and so on) to physical ability and varying levels of individual musical familiarity and preference. Needless to say, the topic is too large to address adequately within the confines of this chapter. Instead, we will discuss aspects of musical knowing related to participation within a community choir.

As an educator, performer and conductor, my (Francesca) experiences tell me that musical knowing is based on experience. It is a knowledge which surpasses notes and rests (musical script for pitches and silence), and instead lies in the realms of the emotion, expression, imagination, spirituality, culture and energy inherent in musical participation. Involvement with music is a way of creating culture, a way of sharing one's self and merging with others to form a new space for those involved.

The development of such spaces can be clearly illustrated in the community choir environment. Interaction in ensembles such as these demonstrates the social nature of music, as well as the potential to foster empathy and understanding of those around you. One of the key facets of musical knowing is identity. Participants (both performers and audience members) enter into the situation with a prior sense of identity. Often, due to personal and cultural influences, individuals identify more with some musical genres than with others, and expect 'like' individuals to do the same. However, when one enters into the realm of a community choir, her/his sense of self is likely to evolve. One may be challenged by the actions or position another member takes, or how one's carefully held preconceptions turn out to be completely inaccurate.

Choirs, especially those with a social justice itinerary, tend to be based on solidarity, trust and collective responsibility (Bogdan 1995, Holmquist 1995). Audience participation (singing/dancing/clapping), walking among the audience, mixing voice parts and converging around important community issues are just some of the ways in which choirs build unity. McCarthy (1999) emphasises the value of live performance, indicating its ability to illuminate shared ideals and commitments. Music, particularly song, is a familiar and accessible medium that can transcend boundaries and communicate with people from other communities.

This communication relies on participants' ability to make meaning of their musical experiences (Bell, 2004). For some, it may be the moment that breath, word and energy all come together; for others, it may be the sight of a dissimilar group moving as one. For many, music engagement is immersion in and personal connection to the immediate. Music as a way of knowing and meaning-making is influenced by physiology, emotion, and the unique language of this art form.

Dimensions of song

Singing is more than just the physical, vocal production of sounds that carries pitches through the air; it is a manifestation of emotion, thought, spirituality and physicality that binds us all as human beings. It is also one of the oldest forms of musical communication in everything from religious practices to entertainment to education. But what is it that makes song such a powerful force across cultures and times?

One area of research has focused on the body's physiological response to singing and song. Couched in scientific and medical terminology, the focus is often on the production of sound (body mechanics, breathing, tone modification, auditory response, and so on), and is discussed in terms of vibration, pitch, frequency and cardiophysical response. It has been proven by countless researchers, including Bartlett (1996), Gomez and Danuser (2004) and Nyklicek, Thayer and Van Doornen (1997), that music elicits measurable effects on the body. Heart and respiratory rates correlate directly to the arousal level of the music; simply, music with faster tempo, louder volume, driving rhythms and dramatic changes resulted in higher heart and respiratory rates, while more restive, sedate pieces revealed the opposite.

These studies also revealed that a person's skin (the largest sensory organ) is affected by musical factors. Have you ever had the hair on your neck stand up or got the chills from a particular musical passage? It is quite possible that the layers of your dermis are responding to the same musical elements which increase your cardiorespiratory rates. Gomez and Danuser (2004) found that the level of skin conductance was linked with the arousal level of the music; the higher the arousal level of the music the higher the skin conductance level.

Relating directly to this research is the relationship between the physiological response and emotion. Classical Greek thought held that certain sounds or pitches could educe specific emotions or moral behaviours. Today, science is attempting to link the body's physical reaction with its emotional one. Moving beyond the relationship between pitch and specific emotion, studies seek to combine the impact of physiology, imagery and the subsequent emotional response. Nyklicek *et al.* (1997) found that music was capable of inducing a wide variety of affective and bodily reactions. Increased tempo (musical speed) for example, tends to be associated with joy or agitation and can produce increased heart rate and breath flow. Imagery in music also plays a role, intensifying both emotional and physiological responses (Nyklicek *et al.*, 1997). Thus song with its embedded musical and textual images offers a potentially powerful emotional and physical stimulant for both performers and audiences alike. Yet, as Magolda (1995) noted, musical communication must extend beyond emotion:

> Participants recognised that connecting to their emotions was essential in deciding what to believe, yet were aware that this had to be balanced with rational reflection. Contextual knowing emphasised that dialogue,

or access to others' perspectives and experiences were required for developing beliefs (p. 149).

Communicative styles of music

Through music, people share ideas, culture, language and stories. Communication through music can be described in three general categories: communication through language, communication through emotion and communication through musical structure.

Musical communication through language involves the literal transfer of ideas via actual words or relationship to the topic. Identification of content and meaning is tangible through listening, performance and/or analysis of text. This literal use of music, or in the case of a community choir, song, is the most common approach to communication through music. Performers and listeners alike are able to comprehend and participate in the verbal message relayed through the music. Social justice choirs are selective in their choice of music, often reflecting on the implications of their music, as well as the possible outcomes.

But the impact of song goes far beyond the power of the word; it also speaks to the soul. Often described in relation to its ability to influence and elicit emotional response, song has the capacity to reach across cultural boundaries and articulate the human experience. Juslin and Laukka (2003) studied the accuracy of the transmission of emotion (via vocal expression and musical performance) across cultures and found that there was a high level of cross-cultural congruence. Not surprisingly, the highest levels of emotional correspondence were found among particular cultural groups. This clearly denotes the influence music can have when attempting to build solidarity or empathy around a socially important cause, but also calls for an awareness of the possibility of division. Many social issues are emotionally charged, highly volatile subjects which need to be approached carefully. Community choir is a site where performers can examine and discuss their own emotional reaction to the music, and the group, before sharing it with an audience.

Communication through musical structure is also integral to this process. There are several elements to include when considering this aspect of a choir. Musicians generally describe 'structure' in terms of musical elements, like voicing, shape of the line(s), contrasting timbres, and so on. These aspects are very important, since attention to these details greatly enhance the overall transmission of the message and musicality of the performance. For example, increasing dynamics (like volume and musical effects) as the line (usually melody) ascends is a very simple way to utilise musical structure to emphasise a point. Often, the text peaks where the melody reaches its highest point. Likewise, contrasting dynamics accentuate areas of significance.

Composition of the ensemble is also a crucial structural issue, especially for a choir focused upon social justice. Everything from repertoire to dress to physical placement of performers can strengthen or detract from the overall statement. For instance, the *Syracuse Community Choir* is comprised of a broad slice of the local population, resulting in a racially, culturally and ethnically diverse group. Of particular note is the inclusion of some severely developmentally disabled individuals and a wide distribution in ages. The objective of director Karen Mihalyi was to 'intentionally seek out kinds of people who might not be represented well in the choir' (Bogdan, 1995, p. 143). The difficult work of full inclusion in the weekly work of the choir is described further on. But in terms of communication to audiences, the visual as well as aural representation of such diversity demands care not only in choosing texts, but in arranging singers, listeners and space. The goal is full and equitable participation of all.

Communication through musical structure ultimately is about who is included in the audience as well as in the choir. Choral music, like many forms of so-called classical music, is historically associated with hushed concert halls or churches and a repertoire that may be criticised for reproducing middle class values and cultural tastes. In contrast, community choirs usually strive to bring music to community gatherings, and to present music that amplifies or stimulates listener engagement in issues that challenge the status quo. We describe a few specific examples in the next sections.

Ensemble dynamics of musical participation

For many, music is viewed as an esoteric art. Its language is unfamiliar, and its performers are believed to require special talent and years of study. Sadly, many adults have decided (or been told) that they 'cannot' sing: and they have accordingly silenced their own voices. Musical participation thus offers the opportunity to reclaim one's voice, in a political act of resistance to the mass production of pleasantly homogeneous popular music. The community choir movement has set out to help adults rediscover joy and confidence in singing and the personal sense of empowerment that one's own voice is valuable.

One example is the *Gettin' Higher Choir* in Victoria, British Columbia, which 'seeks to re-integrate singing into the daily routines of life' (Shivon, 2005, p. 1, 4). Started in 1997, the group now numbers about 250 voices and is led by Shivon Robinsong and Denis Donnelly. No auditions are used, and no ability is required to read music or produce song in a particular way. In fact, Robinsong particularly welcomes those who think they cannot hold a tune, and Donnelly declares one of the 'Rules for Ensemble Singing' to be 'a wrong note sung with authority is an interpretation' (Donnelly, 2005, p. 1). Singers learn to become comfortable with the sound of their own voices through humming together, experimenting with different notes and combinations, playing with volume and colour, listening and throwing back sounds. Tunes and harmony can be learned through this sort of echoing, known as call-and-response style. In one workshop led by Robinsong and Donnelly, Tara watched as over 300 people who had never before sung together (many were firmly convinced of their non-singer status and had to be coaxed to make any sound at all) were singing rich harmonies and complex syncopated rhythms within 30 minutes. Participants were smiling; singing out loud with no visible self-consciousness. Later, some remarked on how 'good' it felt to sing. They said they felt energised and alert, likely not just from the increased oxygen and neural blood flow from the expansive breathing, but also from the intense imaginative concentration and aural stimulation. The leaders continued to emphasise listening: to the individual sounds of the voices on either side, to the rich overall vocal blends, and to one's own voice as a unique contribution to that blend. It is hard to describe the sensation of taking part in filling a large space with big warm harmonies:

moving as one with the voices of all those surrounding you, utterly immersed in the energy and expression of the collective as it climbs vocal lines and senses tempo changes together. This is the magical experience of ensemble, and it is powerful learning about community. As Robinsong declares, 'singing is our birthright; an essential activity for personal and community health and vitality' (Shivon, 2005, p. 11).

Music's ambivalent role in social justice learning

Clearly the experience of music as a holistic way of learning that is uniquely embodied and emotional is well-established, despite its relative marginalisation in mainstream adult education debates. It is interesting to speculate why music may not be so well recognised in promoting social justice as other arts, by adult education research and theory. Perhaps the actual content of music is difficult to analyse: few non-musicians understand its vocabulary and logic sufficiently to theorise its potential interrelation with research, learning or social justice. In addition, instrumental music does not position itself directly as commentary, and concert-style songs (opera, lieder) rarely explicitly address social justice themes. This leaves popular songs, which are to concert music what quilts are to painting in the debates about what constitutes art (Felshin, 1995). Yet most will acknowledge the powerful role in historical social movements of popular protest anthems such as *Blowin' in the wind* or *We shall overcome* and classical musical activists such as Bob Dylan and Joan Baez. More recently we can hear social justice musicians such as anti-globalisation singer Stephen Smith, anti-racism hip hop artist Boots Riley, and country musician James McMurtry singing to protest the Iraq war, homelessness and other social problems. In Canada rap artist K'Nan sings of the destruction of Somalia, K-Os about poverty and violence in north Toronto, and indigenous musicians are using music to revive their own culture and language.[1]

Just what such songs lend to social justice movements and critical social learning in general is hard to pin down. Some like Chang (2002) argue that the social importance of protest music has been muted in recent decades, partly because it bears little effect on policy change. Arguably more so than visual art forms, the commodified construction and distribution of popular music has become increasingly complex, so that these songs cannot be analysed separately from their economic production and manipulation by powerful agendas in mass media. Despite all of this, music undeniably stirs emotion and enables a collective expression; it can bind individuals, mobilise identification, and stir the emotional energy that catalyses and sustains action. Krajnc (2000) is among those who maintain that 1960s songs helped spread progressive ideas into mass culture and drew attention to the Vietnam War, women's issues, and the nuclear debate. She also shows that the next wave of music in social justice was mass events such as the 1980s Live-Aid/Band-Aid concerts with large reach to otherwise inattentive public audiences through mass communication media. Certainly Bob Geldof's 2005 success, focusing media coverage on huge Live-Aid concerts to concentrate public attention again on Africa's oppression and famine, testifies to the powerful potential of music amplified through mass media to push a message.

Krajnc (2000) argues that for progressive social learning that has real impact on civil society, arts must be teamed with the 'media mind-bomb', which has agenda-setting power and ability to change world-views and behaviour. But she adds, in her third dimension of an arts-infused social learning model, that art must also be generated in opportunities for people's personal participation if they are to be truly mobilised to feel, think and act differently. Overall, Krajnc claims, music is under-appreciated in its critical roles which link culture and learning for social change.

Yet music shares with other arts the unique contributions to learning that Butterwick and Dawson (2006) claim are key to democracy. Arts awaken personal creativity, encourage wide and inclusive participation, and provoke radical visions of an alternate world: arts mobilise ordinary people to create for their community a voice, collective identity, and development (Butterwick & Dawson, 2006). Clearly music offers these possibilities for new visions, expanded voices and democratic participation. Community choirs, our focus in this article, include groups such as the *Gettin' Higher Choir* and members of the peace choir movement in Canada such as *Spirit's Call Choir* in Manitoba, as well as, in the US, *Mystic Chorale, Rainbow Chorus, One Voice, Concord Choirs, Sacred Fire,* and *Laughing Spirit,* the *Sheffield Socialist Choir* in England, and *Trots Allt* in Sweden. All share a commitment to inclusion, community building, and social change. These radical community choirs can be viewed as collectives whose members learn solidarity through the experience of writing and singing social justice music, and teach others by sharing their music personally. The *Syracuse Community Choir* in rural New York, which we referred to earlier, was begun in 1985 to sing songs of peace and social justice at community events such as Earth Day, Aids Survivor benefit, International Women's Day. Its special focus is inclusion, integrating persons with physical and developmental disabilities as well as members mixing among ethnic and class groups. According to the director, the important learning is working through all the issues related to diversity; building inclusive community is difficult, uncomfortable and continuous work:

> The choir is about singing and it is about community. The two things go together. By being together and creating a sense of doing something together community begins to form. It is also what the audience feels when it is with us – community. We do a lot of community building in our concerts. Sing alongs and other stuff. We sing about oppression (Bogdan, 2005, p. 33).

In Canada, an example is the *Common Thread Community Chorus of Toronto*, a 70-voice, multicultural, non-audition choir formed in 1999 that describes itself as promoting social justice and community through music. It declares its aim as presenting 'songs that reflect the real lives of ordinary people and speak to the "full cup of life" – birth, death, joy, sorrow, struggle, triumph, work, play, love, community, celebration' (Common Thread, 2005, p. 72).

The emphasis here is less on political change and more on cultural diversity reflected in its musical content and membership. One of their songs is *Torn Screen Door* by David Francey (2005, p. 1) depicting the hardship of Canadian farmers:

> Had a life that they tried to save/ But the banks took it all away Hung a sign on a torn screen door/ Nobody lives here no more They worked their fingers/ To the bone / Nothing left / They can call their own . . .

A more radical and informal group in Edmonton Alberta, the *Notre Dames des Bananas* choir has been performing songs of peace, freedom and equality since it began in the early 1980s. Its website declares that 'members are from diverse backgrounds and include different political philosophies – communist, anarchist, social democrat, green, but all are firmly committed to struggles against a rapacious capitalism' (Notres Dames, 2005, p. 11). Billing itself as the only left-wing, radical choir in Alberta, *Notre Dames des Bananas* sings on picket lines, political rallies and community celebrations such as organised labour's May Week. Its songs are intended to explicitly name forces of oppression and to help mobilise solidarity among listeners: to challenge corporate power, government inaction on social issues, and human rights abuses. Some are classic labour songs found by choir members, and others are written by individual or group members.

Trots allt is an explicitly radical Swedish choral group that originated in 1968 among a group of university students concerned about impending cuts to the social welfare system. This was a period when many social justice choirs emerged in Sweden, and student protests were being staged across Europe initiated by the May uprising in Paris. While many of these radical choirs in Sweden eventually declined, *Trots allt* has sung continuously over the past 35 years, today numbering about 25 members – at least 10 of whom have been with the group since its origins – singing in four parts. The group's name *Trots allt* ('in spite of everything') is a play on words, and the choir continues to write its own lyrics to well-known songs that 'spite' policies and conditions it wishes to protest. Anna Holmgren, one of *Trots allt's* long-term members, explains that the group meets weekly in members' homes. Together the members explore social-political issues, then play with music. The choir presents its songs without charge for political meetings, for labour gatherings, and for the community (personal communication, 19 August, 2005). During the referendum for the European Union for example, *Trots Allt* toured meetings singing its satirical lyrics to the popular song *Embrace Me* to drum up anti-EU sentiment:

> Let me in you are my hope and my everything,
> I want to rest in your arms, your embrace makes me so beautiful and rich.
> Towards a united future the road is safe, I am blindly in love ..."
> (Holmgren, 2005)

The group deliberately tries to raise critical awareness and provoke community attention to social problems. These range from increased multinational ownership and unemployment to the treatment of refugees in Sweden. Satire is their trademark. Here are their lyrics to *Vem du än är* (*Whoever you are* – English translation by Anna Holmgren), about the hardships of new immigrants:

> Whoever you are, you can be happy you made it,
> Here you may live in barracks, in the country(side) –
> you get a quick lesson in our language, you get orders not to start a fight.
> So hear us / you should be grateful you could cross the border.
> Maybe you will make it in the competition/ the market in the world
> is now in rule / It is good at "people-taming" . . . (Holmgren, 2005)

In each of these examples, musical participation emphasises slightly different purposes of social justice. In the *Syracuse Community Choir*, the meaning of diversity in community is continually fore-grounded through deliberate inclusion of differently-abled members who might normally be excluded from a performing choir. The choral requirement of close listening to one another and achieving collective harmony demands an intimacy that forces people to confront and work through tensions of difference at very personal levels. The *Common Thread Community Chorus* similarly emphasises community-building in the actual experience of choral participation, through its multi-ethnic membership and its songs focusing on the everyday stories of people's lives within social structural inequities. *Notres Dames des Bananes* and *Trots Allt* focus more on provocation of the external community through their own musical creations presenting radical social critiques.

But in all four choirs, critical education occurs both internally and externally, through both the singing process and the content of songs for social justice. The singers, whether they actually create the songs or not, learn in the very process of participating together to plumb the spirit of a song's message, then develop musical expression that engages listeners. In this engagement, listeners learn through an immersion in sound that moves emotions of outrage and longing, rouses critical awareness at deep levels of being, and opens imaginations to new possibilities.

Recommendations for adult educators

Song provides adult education with an effective pedagogical medium, one that does not require years of training or special aptitude. Instead, it calls for educators to approach their content area with a critical eye and a keen understanding of the intricacies of social relationships. In my (Francesca's) experience, music, especially song, has been proven to enhance the educational experience of many adult learners, regardless of format or mode. Adult educators could incorporate music into their educational activities in four ways: subservient integration; co-equal cognitive integration style; affective style of integration; and social integration (Bresler, cited in Mark, 2002). Each method creates the opportunity for group discussion and allows for new insight about and/or reinforcement of the learning objective.

By far, the most common educational use of music is subservient integration, or the directly referential use of music. Instructors arrange learners' engagement in music presenting stories or commentary extending the issue under study. Learners need encouragement to develop personal and critical responses, to analyse their own and appreciate others' responses, and to reflect on not just the song's text but its musical dimensions contributing to its communicative power.

Another pedagogical approach is what some musicians call the co-equal cognitive integration style. This involves both the teacher and the students analysing the relationship of the music to the topic. This moves the learners beyond the literal word to what is implied or represented by musical content: examining effect of melody, of rhythm, and of instrumentation on the message. Popular sings and music scores in film clips can be analysed for their intended and actual emotional effects. Further, these sometimes invoke ironic commentary or problematic representations. The film music for *Dangerous Minds* starring Michelle Pfeiffer, for example, can be critically analysed for creating cultural hierarchies and racist stereotypes. Tinari and Khandke (2000) describe using music to teach economics. By analysing songs they self-selected, students were able to glean not only concepts about economics, but also about the interrelationship between their area of study and other aspects of their lives. These uses of music are most effective when the texts chosen/ performances attended address social justice issues. Educators should encourage critical, democratic dialogue among the learners. This should encompass not only the subject at hand, but also the choice of musical venue and inclusion (or exclusion) of specific works. Discussions should involve the recognition of what may not have been represented musically, as well as how these musical ideas may comment on other facets of social life.

The third style, the affective style, involves using music to stimulate a mood: music listening or singing can relax, energise, create humour and induce nostalgia. Dialogue can allow learners to begin to critically examine their responses to music and compare their own to others' responses. Analysis can extend to songs comprising learners' environments, from radio to grocery-store muzak, and examine the effects on one's identity, values, and choices.

Actual singing activity is an important approach to the fourth style of using music in education: social integration. Here, music is actually used as a means to create a community. This requires an attention to detail, realisation of the complexities of sociocultural factors, and the need to facilitate the process, not control it. Francesca once attended a workshop where everyone began by singing 'Good morning!' in their own language, then sang again to one another in a language different from their first. We each had to listen closely to one another and think as a group. The shared experience of humour, struggle, insight, and discomfort created a bond between us that carried through the entire workshop.

Educators themselves can lead singing, or local community choir directors are often approachable to conduct workshops or class visits to create this experience. Actually participating in community song – rediscovering one's voice and confronting one's fears and pleasures in using it – is a very effective way to open dialogue about the power and the suppression of our authentic voices in contemporary Western culture.

Olsen (2003) observed that 'Music can allow individuals to view life more critically, challenging assumptions and biased values that they came to regard as accepted reality through their own community experience' (p. 113). Singing is a powerful medium through which we can learn, confront hegemonic power structures, reclaim all voices to build inclusive communities, and confront social concerns.

Conclusion

We have focused in this article on music in general and community choral singing in North America and Europe particular. We have shown that people actually make meaning and communicate meaning in unique ways through the poetry of song and the experience of singing. The physiological dynamics of singing: of merging one's breathing with the rhythms and arc of a musical phrase, of virtually taking the tune simultaneously into one's lungs and ears, is an experience that weds spirit, body, emotion and imagination. To be surrounded by the sound of others, vocalising precisely the same message simultaneously, listening intently to all while being listened to, is a powerful relational encounter of transcendence and solidarity. The community learning offered by community choirs such as those we have profiled here is also unique. These choirs deliberately set out to mix people of diverse social groups and ability to foreground the process of learning how to be in community.

In an art form that has garnered a reputation for exclusion through its esoteric language and virtuosity, community choirs subvert conventional notions of musical 'talent' to include everyone as full participants. We have also argued that participation in the creative processes of writing social justice songs and music as well as preparing their musical expression constitutes important critical learning. And finally, the content of the songs themselves engages audiences in confronting conditions of inequity and injustice, envisioning alternate possibilities, and daring to consider their personal responsibility. This message is not unlike the offerings of visual arts, dance and drama in social justice: but music engages listeners through the unique medium of tune, harmony and rhythm, stirring people at deep levels which somehow lie beyond visual and poetic imagination.

Acknowledgements

This chapter has been amended, updated and revised based on the article 'Pedagogies of Song: Music as/in Adult Education' published in the *Pennsylvania Association for Adult and Continuing Education Journal.*

Notes

[1] We are indebted to Editor Darlene E. Clover for drawing our attention to the work of Felshin and Canadian rap artists.

References

Bartlett, D. L. (1996) 'Physiological responses to music and sound stimuli'. In D. A. Hodges, (ed), *Handbook of music psychology* (pp. 343–85). San Antonio: IMR Press.

Baxter Magolda, M. (1995) 'The integration of relational and impersonal knowing in young adults' epistemological development', *Journal of College Student Development*, Vol. 36, No. 3, pp. 205–16.

Bell, C. L. (2004) 'Update on community choirs and singing in the United States', *International Journal of Research in Choral Singing*, Vol. 2, No. 1, pp. 29–52.

Bogdan, R. (1995) 'Singing for an inclusive society: The community choir'. In S. J. Taylor, R. Bogdan and Z. M. Lutfiyya (eds), *The variety of community experience: Qualitative studies of family and community life* (pp. 141–54). Baltimore: Paul H. Brookes.

Bogdan, R. (2005) *The community choir: Singing for an inclusive society*. Retrieved July 20, 2005 from http://thechp.syr.edu/choir.htm

Butterwick, S. and Dawson, J. (2006) 'About education and the arts'. In T. Fenwick, B. Spencer & T. Nesbit (eds), *Contexts of adult education: Canadian perspectives*. Toronto: Thompson.

Chang, J. (2002) 'Is protest music dead?' *Counterpunch*, April 2, 2002. Retrieved on July 16, 2007 from http://www.counterpunch.org/changprotestmusic.html

Common Thread (2005) Home page of Common Thread Community Chorus. Retrieved on August 31, 2005 from http://commonthread chorus.ca

Donnelly, D. (2005) Rules for ensemble singing. Retrieved on October 15, 2005 from http://www.crucible.ca/ghc/4/rules_for_ensemble _singing.htm

Felshin, N. (ed) (1995) *But is it art? The spirit of art as activism*. Seattle: Bay Press.

Francey, D. (2005) *Torn screen door*. Retrieved on September 25, 2005 from http://www.davidfrancey.com/lyrics_tsd.html

Gomez, P. and Danuser, B. (2004) 'Affective and physiological responses to environmental noises and music', *International Journal of Psycho-physiology*, Vol. 53, pp. 91–103.

Holmgren, A. (2005) Personal communication to Tara Fenwick (email), September 20, 2005.

Holmquist, S. P. (1995) *A study of community choir members' experiences*. Un-published doctoral dissertation, University of Oregon, Eugene, Oregon.

Juslin, P. N. and Laukka, P. (2003) 'Communication of emotions in vocal expression and music performance: Different channels, same code?' *Physiological Bulletin*, Vol. 129, No. 5, pp. 770–814.

Kaltoft, G. (1999) *Music and emancipatory learning in three community education programs*. Unpublished doctoral dissertation, Teachers College, Columbia University, New York.

Krajnc, A. (2000) 'The art of green learning: From protest songs to media mind bombs', *International Politics*, Vol. 37, No. 1, pp. 19–40.

Mark, M. L. (2002) 'Nonmusical outcomes of music education: Historical considerations'. In R. Colwell & C Richardson (eds), *The new handbook of research on music teaching and learning* (pp. 1045–52). New York: Oxford University Press.

McCarthy, M. (1999) *Passing it on: The transmission of music in Irish culture*. Cork: Cork University Press.

Notres Dames (2005) Homepage of Notres Dames des Bananes, Edmonton, Alberta. Retrieved on August 30, 2005 from http://www.notre damedesbananes.ca

Nyklicek, I., Thayer, J. F. and Van Doornen, L. J. P. (1997) 'Cardio-respiratory differentiation of musically-induced emotions', *Journal of Psychophysiology*, Vol. 11, No. 4, pp. 304–21.

Olsen, K.R. (2003) *Bridge over troubled water: Exploring music's role in building communities of adult learners*. Unpublished doctoral dissertation, National Louis University.

Shaw, M. and Martin, I. (2005) 'Translating the art of citizenship', *Convergence*, Vol. 38, No. 4, pp. 85–100.

Shivon (2005) Homepage of Shivon Robinsong, Gettin' Higher Choir. Retrieved on October 1, 2005 from http://www.shivon.com/Shivon/NewFiles/ghc.html

Tinari, F. D. and Khandke, K. (2000) 'From rhythm and blues to Broadway: Using music to teach economics', *Journal of Economic Education*, Vol. 31, No. 3, pp. 253–70.

CHAPTER 8

Weaving community

Social and economic justice
in the mountains

Penne Lane

Introduction

Contemplating the interrelated nature of social justice and the arts begins by clarifying the definition of social justice. I understand it to be any concerted effort to address the social, cultural and economic inequities that are rapidly spreading throughout the world. The arts – both traditional and contemporary – are often a means for local communities to prosper from the increasingly interconnected global economy. International aid agencies and non-governmental organisations realise this and often address the educational and economic needs of local communities through arts related initiatives. A special report from UNESCO (2003) recognised that development and educational efforts must be 'strategically designed to have an impact on the economic life of people in general and of the poor and disadvantaged in particular' (p. 2). More often than not, as Myles Horton once noted, social justice is economic justice (in Jacobs, 2003).

Much has been written about the social and cultural changes in communities and families when women in developing countries undertake handicraft production to supplement their incomes (Ehlers, 1990; Nash, 1992. Little is known, however, about these transitions in the countries of the former Soviet Union. The Carpathian mountain region of western Ukraine is very similar to the southern Appalachian

165

mountain region in the eastern United States. Both have distinct cultures with rich handicraft traditions. In this chapter I discuss how in both of these contexts, consumer education, marketing strategies, and regional policy advocacy can combine with traditional and contemporary arts to work towards greater economic justice for rural communities.

Appalachian handicraft producers learned long ago how to employ the arts in local economic development efforts. There is currently a large body of literature focusing on southern Appalachian cultural traditions and hand crafts (Whisnant, 1983; Ehler, 1995; Williams, 2002). Supportive legislation, the work of NGOs, and influential individuals contributed to a successful revival of traditional handicraft in the Appalachian region. The institutional support is essential; however, equally important is a tradition of maintaining kinship and close social relations that sustains people and helps pass skills from one generation to the next.

However, the Appalachian handicraft revival had many exploitive aspects (Becker, 1998) as mass production techniques turned artisans into cogs in the wheels of industrial manufacturers. Yet some individuals have reclaimed control of these development processes and slowly created a handicraft revival sensitive to and respectful of artisans. Adapting local traditions to outside market demands taught Appalachian artisans a great deal that may inform development processes among Carpathian mountain handicraft producers. It is important to note, however, that the creation of a uniquely Ukrainian form of economic development adds to our understanding of what a more sustainable process could look like.

In this chapter I use the metaphor of a four-harness loom to discuss several frameworks that influence the lives of artisans at regional, community and individual levels. To understand the context of these community-based economic development efforts, I begin with a strong warp: a brief background of Ukrainian independence and images of the Appalachian handicraft revival efforts. These will illustrate how individuals, supported by strong social networks and regional initiatives, have facilitated arts-based development. As the more decorative weft, I present the stories of individuals and communities from both the Carpathians and the southern Appalachian mountains to illustrate the interwoven nature of local and regional development processes. Through this comparison, we will begin to understand the intersections of historical context, life experiences, and contemporary social and cultural transformations as individuals adapt to political, social and economic changes. Much of this research is drawn from ten years of collaboration with a regional development initiative in the southern Appalachian region. Personal correspondence over the last four years with an artist from the Carpathian mountain region of western Ukraine, Tanya (a pseudonym), and a site evaluation visit to Ukraine in the spring of 2004 inform my understanding.

A four-harness loom

The complex web of adaptations utilised in community development initiatives is similar to the process of weaving on a four-harness loom. This loom has four heddles like wide, thin picture frames located one behind the other. Hundreds of small wires or strings divide each heddle. A skilled weaver must painstakingly thread each piece of the warp between selected wires or strings to create the intricate patterns of, for example, a traditional Appalachian coverlet. Once threaded, each harness/heddle can raise or lower its set of warp threads as the weaver carefully manipulates the weft thread back and forth on the loom.

The warp, the threads placed on a loom to form the background of the weaving, is much like the historical context of a community that forms the background upon which the patterns of individual lives are produced. The heddles form frames around various aspects of the weaving just as contemporary political and economic structures form frames around individuals and institutions that make up that community. Each weaver chooses which frame to raise so that intersections form between various threads. Similarly, individuals express human agency as they interpret and manipulate various aspects of the frames that affect their lives. Like skilled artisans, individuals weave their life experiences in and around the political and economic changes of their day-to-day lives. Doing this they create a fabric of social connections, an intricate weaving like an Appalachian coverlet or a beautiful Carpathian wool rug.

The warp: historical context

Kyiv occupies the central region of Ukraine with the Dnieper River dividing the country evenly between east and west. Kravchuck (2002) describes Ukraine as 'subjected to a damaging economic colonisation during the years of Soviet rule' (p. 2).The east was heavily industrialised and populated predominantly by people who saw themselves as culturally and ethnically Russian. The west, however, 'has remained a bastion of intense nationalistic sentiment' (p. 2) as the majority of people cling to their traditional Ukrainian heritage among the foothills of the Carpathian Mountains.

Following World War II the western region experienced a collective nightmare as Josef Stalin sought to install the Russian culture and a communist economic system. Women were expected to participate in building the communist state which was to provide for everyone's well-being equally, although in reality the shortage economy kept everyone equally poor. Care for the elderly was provided through pensions and children were cared for in state-funded centres. As elsewhere in the world, however, women continued to bear the burden of the double shift, maintaining households and caring for families in addition to a full day's work for paid wages.

The Appalachian region is also defined along political and economic lines while culturally it follows the mountains running south to north inland from the eastern shores of the mid- to southern United States. Towards the end of the nineteenth century, technological advances allowed industrial developers to exploit the natural resources. Throughout the early years of the twentieth century these absentee landowners employed local mountain people in timber and coal mining at barely liveable wages, paid them in company script (money substitutes) that could only be used in company-owned stores, and forced them to live in company-owned tenement houses (Ehler, 1995). The people lived by subsistence farming and practised handicraft production for their own use and for sale within the region. Coal and timber were extracted from the region by railway and highway to support the expanding industrial development in the north-eastern US. Life in the traditional Appalachian culture was physically demanding and financially stressful. The extremely high unemployment rates in the region combined with the acquiescence of workers and power of local elites to encourage outside investment (Gaventa, 1982).

Soon after the natural resource base neared depletion, investors from outside the region began to take advantage of cheap labour and limited union protection of workers. The region supported hundreds of sewing factories, furniture manufacturing facilities and later, electronics production industries. It was the site of the earliest and most bitter labour strikes in the country as workers demanded social protections, fair wages, and other benefits. Women constituted a majority of the workforce in the sewing, light manufacturing and cottage industries of the region. In both Ukraine and in Appalachia, the general perception is that women provide primarily a supplemental income. The reality has been that many of these women are heads of households and they have been devastated by the loss of employment resulting from economic transitions.

A knot in the thread: The collision of tradition and modernity

During the later part of the rule of Imperial Russia, which included much of the territory of present day Ukraine, a revival of cultural traditions accompanied a 'collision of tradition and modernity' (Salmond, 1996, p. 1). The symphonies and ballets that came to represent the region had been preserved through the years, but 'one thread has gradually been dropped from the colourful fabric of cultural expression' (Salmond, 1996, p. 1). That thread was the handicraft traditions of the kustar, the peasants of Ukraine and Russia. This revival has been compared to the European Arts and Crafts movement that resulted from a search for alternatives to the growing mechanisation and industrialisation of later nineteenth century life. Much like its western European counterpart, this revival was paternalistic and involved many unintended consequences as the westernised elite arranged for formally-trained artists to teach folk art to the folk. Schools were started on the estates of wealthy benefactors supported primarily by the women of the merchant and noble classes. In the social context of the time 'the arenas of charitable good works and the decorative arts were both considered acceptable spheres of activity for ladies' (Salmond, 1996, p. 9), and women from the Momontov family of Moscow and artist, Elena Polenova, invested time and talent in the production of kustar crafts. One of the most successful aspects of this revival was the development of an export market for these sometimes roughly constructed products. This market, used to create a sense of national pride in the people, served political and economic purposes contributing to an economic revival among the poorest in the region.

Women, particularly the wealthier class, have often reacted to the social and economic inequities created by industrialisation by supporting philanthropic efforts that, like the kustar revival, sought alternatives. During the early part of the twentieth century, similar concerns brought prosperous young women from the more developed north-eastern US into the Appalachian Mountains seeking alternatives and involvement in social justice work. Olive Dame Campbell and her husband were amongst the earliest of these well-intentioned educators to travel throughout the southern Appalachian region and document the cultural and economic situation. Once in the region, they found weavers, basket makers, potters and woodcarvers producing handicrafts that reflected the abundant natural resources and rich cultural heritage of the region.

After the death of her husband, Olive Dame Campbell travelled to Denmark to study the Danish Folk Schools built around the preservation of cultural traditions and handicrafts. Returning to Appalachia, she built the John C. Campbell Folk School on land donated by local farmers. The first teachers were traditional crafts women and men she found working in the area. Contributions from educational foundations and well-intentioned individuals provided materials for the school. Campbell and others worked to create awareness of the economic situation in the Appalachian region and to develop new markets for fine handicrafts.

A contemporary heddle: Weaving a life in changing times

Ukraine's record of economic transition is 'an abysmal one' (Kravchuk, 2002, p. 3). Just prior to Ukrainian independence in 1991, women made up 70–80 per cent of the total unemployment figures throughout the Soviet Union (Attwood, 1996). The contemporary tax structure in Ukraine can take as much as 50 per cent of a business's income. Socio-economic transitions that began during the final days of the Russian rule forced many, predominantly women, into informal economic situations where individuals rely on social networks and kinship relations, and often exchange goods on the barter system. Combined with a burdensome licensing system and rampant corruption, individual artisans simply could not afford to move into the formal economy so many can be found in the informal economy which although not considered illegal, carries on outside the tax-based, formal economy. This informal sector employment provides desperately needed cash income, but seldom offers any social protections such as job security, a living wage, or health care provisions.

A market at Kosov (photographed by P. Lane)

Artisans in the Carpathians sell their products in the market at Kosov rather than transport goods to large cities where they must rely on intermediaries who add to the cost of doing business. If one views Ukraine as a colony of Russia, contemporary times can be seen as a post-colonial phase lacking sufficient infrastructure, institutions or legislation to provide for adequate economic development. As a result, families and individuals supplement their incomes with various entrepreneurial endeavours just as many women in Appalachia and in other developing countries have always done – with the production and sale of fine handicrafts.

Like Ukraine, the Appalachian region has been colonised by its neighbours to the north. Economic transition in Appalachia received a tremendous boost from the formation of The Appalachian Regional Commission (ARC) in 1965 (Williams, 2002). With a mandate to develop the area and its people, the ARC supported infrastructure such as schools, highways and water treatment facilities. Another federal agency, the Tennessee Valley Authority (TVA) focused efforts on bringing electric power to the region through an extensive system of water- and coal-fired power plants.

More recently, the Appalachian region has seen rising unemployment and underemployment as many of the manufacturing facilities in the region have relocated to other countries. International trade policies like the North American Free Trade Agreement (NAFTA) permit transnational corporations to exploit labour markets around the world. The loud sucking sound that critics of NAFTA claimed would follow the movement of manufacturing was heard loud and clear in the hills of Appalachia. Hard-won protections such as labour rights and environmental regulations have been gutted by neo-conservative policies and education and social services are underfunded in the neo-liberal move to privatisation and market structures. Central Appalachia has a 27 per cent poverty rate and unemployment of around five per cent.

A cultural heddle: Dynamic evolution and multiple traditions

Cultural heritage and traditions define a group of people and sometimes define a region. The western region of Ukraine has a pluralistic heritage with Hungarian, Roma, Jewish, Russian, Polish and Ukrainian cultures intermingled. Cultural traditions in Southern Appalachia are a blend of Scots-Irish heritage from the people that settled the mountains shortly after the American revolutionary war. There is a strong Native American heritage here as well with a tradition of double-weave baskets so finely woven they were used to hold water. The somewhat more limited African American tradition left a strong legacy in the music and dancing of the region.

The Carpathian mountain region is seen by many as a vacation centre and the mineral springs in and around the community of Truskavetz have historically drawn tourists from throughout Eastern Europe. Home to many sanatoriums and health spas, the region's street vendors sell dried mushrooms, local medicinal herbs, and a few handicrafts from the plaza. The focus of the market here is on the health benefits of the natural environment. Through the efforts of local arts supporters, Truskavetz opened a museum dedicated to the famous weaver, Mykailo Bila, who lives in the community. It displays his beautiful tapestries several of which illustrate the craft market at Kosov, but his weavings are pictures in textile rather than utilitarian items such as hand woven rugs or blankets, the crafts of the region.

A deeply religious people for whom orthodox religious iconography continues to be a focus of the arts, Ukrainian women embroider long narrow towels that are draped across pictures of saints and honoured ancestors. The artistic skills exhibited in these beautiful embroideries have seldom been adapted to items that could find a market as anything other than souvenirs, quaint memories of a visit to the Carpathians. In rather romanticised language, Danchenko (1982) notes that the end of tsarist control at the beginning of the nineteenth century 'flung wide open the doors to capitalism in rural areas' (p. 9) and that cottage industries thrived throughout rural communities by the later part of the nineteenth century. Over time, communities such as Kosov became design centres and crafts men and women duplicated work originating in these areas. The bazaar at Kosov is still open and has the feeling of rural bazaars the world over, but the designs of crafts men and women are no longer carried on in contemporary art schools.

The marketing heddle: Hand production or mass production?

The marketing of fine handicrafts has several essential characteristics. Initially and perpetually, there is the slow painstaking, time-consuming process of creating fine handcraft. It stands in fundamental contradiction to the mass production/mass consumption principles of contemporary market economics. Individual agency, the choices we make, carry far-reaching consequences. As artisans choose the creative path, the handmade heritage of fine handcraft production, they often passionately resist mass production. It is seldom a life path that leads to great wealth. Surveys of artisans in the United States indicate the majority of artisans make this choice because of the lifestyle it provides – more time to spend with family, more control over their lives. For many artisans around the world, however, it is a choice made with very limited alternatives.

Another perennial problem for handicraft producers is the limited access to raw materials. In the Kosov market in the Carpathian Mountains, men and women sell beautiful hand carved wooden jewellery. These beautiful pieces sell for incredibly low prices in part because they need minor quality improvements. Bracelets are made with rubber bands and recycled clasps; jewellery is fashioned out of recycled metal wires. Beautiful products could be made even more beautiful, and more valuable, if these artisans had the support of the extensive craft industry available to those in the Appalachian region. The mountains nearby provide adequate wood supplies and inspiration. What these producers lack is peripheral products such as durable threads to string wooden beads together, hinges for the beautiful hand carved boxes or packing supplies and reliable (and affordable) transportation to reach international markets.

Like markets all over the world, the bazaar at Kosov is a place where one can buy virtually anything. Handmade embroideries and fine woven rugs are jammed into outdoor stalls that are little more than plywood tables or wires strung between trees. Next to these items, you may find fresh produce or plastic containers. Recycled old jewellery may sit next to finely carved chess sets and artisans or other family members sell products to retailers from larger cities. Poverty is on display here. Men and women work from dawn to dusk to produce craft items because it is what they know – or what they have access to – while others sell second-hand products brought in, mostly outside the legal, tax-based system, to be traded or sold to neighbours. Mainstream marketing that values low-cost and disposable products discriminates against artisans whose work is the antithesis of mass production.

In the Roaring Creek community of Appalachia, the collaboration of artists and business people has created a different market structure. Drawing on the beautiful autumn colours of the deciduous trees in the National Forests nearby, a fall festival draws thousands of visitors and hundreds of skilled artisans in the region. They are supported by local community development organisations and by an expansive crafts market that provides raw materials, training manuals, and equipment although like in the Ukraine, they are by no means wealthy. However, marketing materials do focus the consumers' understanding on these works as one of a kind, hand crafted items that demand a higher price. Local museums offer visitors a glimpse of the history and culture of the region and local restaurants and rental cabins all collaborate to provide a memorable experience for visitors and a profitable one for local artisans.

The shuttle: Interesting women and individual agency
In weaving, a shuttle carries the weft threads back and forth, over and under the warp threads to form a unified fabric. Like weaving, contemporary realities and changing individual perspectives pass back and forth over the historical context of a community to form the fabric of our

lives. Like a shuttle carrying threads back and forth, a sense of agency gives direction and pattern to our lives. It assists women to make choices about taking action, not being acted upon, and about questioning and challenging the social and economic realities. The women of the kustar revival and the Appalachian folk school movement make choices to be involved in something quite different. They make choices about designs and colours, marketing strategies and the importance of incorporating or ignoring the perspectives of local artisans in their sometimes-grandiose plans for economic revival. The artisans also make choices creating patterns within the community.

Directed by Tanya (a pseudonym), a small group of Ukrainian women produces art products for sale outside the formal, taxed economic system. The women who participate in this group represent a microcosm of the various social groups who are forced out of the formal economy as the country makes the transition to a market system. One is a pensioner whose shrinking state-funded pension will not support her and her family. Another was trained as a paediatrician whose work remains officially, and financially, a part of the failing state apparatus. Like many other professionally-trained women, she cannot survive on the limited pay available as the country shifts state funding to private sources.

Tanya explains, "I've got three children to support!" as she discusses her entrepreneurial efforts. She is a professionally-trained artist whose salary from the art institute fell to nearly nothing in Ukraine's early days of transition. Several years before Ukraine declared independence, Tanya travelled with her husband to the Mediterranean coast of Croatia. Her husband is also an artist and they painted small landscapes and other images from the coast that they sold to tourists in the region. She says, "I sold a small painting for the same amount of money that I earned for a week of teaching at the Institute!" Then she sat and cried asking, "Why does my country have to be like this?" She and her family still travel to the seashore on occasion and she and her husband still sell paintings to support their holiday. Like the majority of Ukrainians, they live in a crowded three-room flat with her husband and three children. They work at least ten hours a day producing crafts to sell to the tourists, and they dream of a beautiful house in the country. It is a dream that I fear will never come true.

The women who work with Tanya produce small pictures made of fused glass and ceramics and they rely on a network of friends and colleagues for materials. When the paediatrician nearly gave up all hope in her desperate financial situation as a professional woman in a crumbling economy, Tanya taught her how to make handmade ceramic beads and these were added to the product line. The beads and pictures are fired in an ancient, tiny electric kiln and Tanya longs for the equipment they need. There is little or no infrastructure to support artisan production. Stains and clay for the beads must come from industrial sources and there is little quality control of products.

In the Appalachians, Linda (pseudonym), who married a fine white oak-basket-maker, was determined to teach consumers to appreciate and respect what she calls "fine hand crafts". She and her husband worked hard to change a perception of craft as being less valuable than the visual arts (e.g. music, literature and theatre) because of its utilitarian nature (Greenhalgh, 1997). These two people collaborated with others from the Roaring Creek community and began to develop businesses around the arts. Through a local community organisation, they established classes to train others in the successful path they had developed. They collaborated with other artists to create sufficient production to attract wholesale and retail buyers to their remote community. They had to be willing to work together and avoid the competition of modern capitalist society.

These two leaders in their small community joined with other local communities to develop a heritage association. The association co-ordinates marketing efforts built on the industrial mining and logging history and the rich handicraft traditions of the region. Economic development capitalises on tourist traffic in the region drawn there initially by the creation of the National Forest and for the fresh air, mineral springs and the natural beauty of the area. Linda and her husband have taught craft skills at the nearby John C. Campbell School that remains a healthy operating folk school after nearly a century of arts education in the region. They have taught classes in both craft skills and the business of art through their local civic organisation. Limited support has come from federal organisations like the ARC, TVA and from state arts and humanities organisations. However, the majority of the work in the area has come through a reliance on social networks and the rich cultural heritage that was the foundation of their success.

A different warp: Development and artisans

The development discourse began at the close of World War II as the dominant states sought to modernise and industrialise the so-called 'South' (Rist, 2002). Early development efforts, nearly always top-down and paternalistic, targeted the countries of Latin America, Africa and Asia and supported the expansion of capitalism and a consumer society. Prior to this growth of international development, extensive efforts to control economics and education in the Southern Appalachians began with the advent of the folk schools. Slightly earlier still, economic development efforts began in rural communities in the Carpathians and surrounding region which focused on the kustar crafts women and men.

Handicraft production efforts have long been a tool of international development professionals. Huseby-Darvas (2001) focused on the social interactions of Hungarian village women who sell wildflowers in regional markets. Humphreys (1999) suggests the more controversial perspective that highlighting labour-intensive handicraft production may contribute to stereotypical perceptions of women as relatively unskilled labour suitable for fine manipulative handwork, and not much else, thereby contributing to low wages and exploitive working conditions. Becker (1998) discusses an aspect of the Appalachian handicraft movement that exploited artisan producers who at times were paid desperately low piece-work wages for production of beautiful crafts that commanded high prices in communities outside the region. Countless other studies relate the complex cultural changes involved as women earn paid wages for handicrafts even as they continue to negotiate social and cultural roles within the family and community (Nash, 1992; Seligmann, 2001; Grimes & Milgram, 2000; Ehlers, 1990).

Development programmes focused on fine handicraft production are most often used in the global South and many rely on international alternative trade organisations (Littrell & Dickson, 1999) to market their products. These organisations rely heavily on volunteer efforts for their marketing and distribution processes and, while they provide much-needed income, products sell for relatively low prices and depend on philanthropic tendencies of the consumer. Many of these handicraft producers remain at the margins of the consumer market relying heavily on the empathy of consumers and producing at the lowest possible cost.

Mainstream economic development efforts force skilled artisans to compromise their products by adopting mass production methods. This can do more than simply alter the products; it compromises the artisan as well. Tanya and many other Ukrainian artists have a good understanding of capitalism referring to it as "Coca Cola". Tanya is a woman who can produce extraordinary paintings and one of a kind works of art, but she says "cats and fishes, cats and fishes" and produces images of cats and fishes because that is what will sell in the limited markets to which she has access. She understands techniques that could greatly expand their production and move her business into the formal economy. But in her self-image, she is an artist first, not a business-woman, a capitalist, or a manufacturer. Is it fair to force these talented artisans to adjust to an economic system that is designed to work against them? Mass production at the lowest cost does not fit the world of fine handicrafts. What right does anyone have to force this conformity, disrespecting the individuals' right to choose? Lacking access to suffici-ent studio space and affordable materials, the work of Tanya and her colleagues is likely to remain in the informal sector and provide little

Hand woven rug (Photographed by P. Lane)

security for her and those who work with her. We do not live in a world where control of our lifestyle is an option if that lifestyle differs greatly from mainstream capitalist production systems.

International trade policies have far-reaching effects on local artisans. Export policies developed in collaboration with the International Monetary Fund and focused on international trade often hinder local artisan production and marketing strategies. The artisans at Kosov market in the Carpathians produce beautiful hand-woven rugs of hand spun wool and yet, the country prohibits the sale of these items through excessive export duties on wool. These export regulations, intended to protect major wool producing countries, affect traditional craftswomen as well. Countries could designate handicrafts as cultural products exempt from such trade regulations and support the development of a crafts industry that could in turn help solve problems of unemployment and underemployment while preserving local cultural traditions.

International development processes become increasingly complicated as macroeconomic policies reach into individual lives at the community level. It is at this level, where local individuals rely on social networks and cultural traditions, that development takes place as 'a multiplicity of new practices that spring forth at the crossroads of history and cultures' (Rist, 2002, p. 138). Development happens in the lives and communities of people in day-to-day struggles in the pursuit of a good education, a decent standard of living, and the right to be creative and productive. During the course of the last decade there was a growing attempt to make development processes more inclusive of local voices and perspectives (Hickey & Mohan, 2004). However, many intergovernmental organisations and international aid agencies are only beginning to understand the complex interactions that take place in local communities at these crossroads of history and culture.

Cut from the same piece of cloth: Patterns for the future
Across time people have sought to preserve the traditions of fine handicraft production; some through the work of social agencies that support the arts, others through acquiring the skills and knowledge needed to produce fine handicraft. Their efforts are woven together to produce beautiful products and healthy communities. Looking at the activities of individuals in these two regions, Carpathian and Appalachian, foregrounds commonalities of artisans everywhere. Both

regions have abundant natural resources and communities of skilled artisans that make use of the materials around them to embellish the things of everyday life. Today both regions face similar economic hardships brought on by globalisation of markets and political changes beyond their control.

Threading the loom, understanding the historical context of a community, provides grounding in local tradition that helps individuals weave their lives in and around the contemporary social and political changes they must face. The folk schools of Appalachia and the kustar revival focused on traditional handicraft to bring renewed respect for local products and the local culture that produced them. The Bila Weaving Museum in the Carpathian Mountains could be used as a focal point for the contemporary weaving traditions in the area, coordinating exhibitions of contemporary weavers and educating the public about the time-consuming process.

Like the communities around Roaring Creek in Appalachia, regional planning agencies in the Carpathians could focus on the development of infrastructure to support artisans and their patrons. As development initiatives learn to listen, communities at the crossroads of history and culture will be empowered to weave new patterns in the fabric of their lives. Adult educators interested in social justice should facilitate these development initiatives, enabling local people in an exploration of the social, political, and economic forces that affect them. Re-valuing the production and marketing of fine handicrafts can create effective economic revitalisation. Artisans are marginalised from the mass-production/mass-consumption economic system. Creating a space for them to work within that system would help create a more just society and perhaps enhance the beauty of everyday things along the way.

Well-known adult educator, Myles Horton, worked in the communities of central Appalachia. His work at Highlander sought the creation of 'a new social order where human values, not property values [would] be supreme' (Jacobs, 2003, p. 213). Horton saw clearly that, more often than not, economic justice is social justice. Through his work at Highlander he sought 'nothing short of a new economic system based upon production for use and not for profit' (2003, p. 214). Fine handicraft producers embellish our lives with production for use. These individuals could be empowered to understand the historical context, the social and cultural interactions that are the threads that bind communities and societies together. What Horton saw as a 'race between social enlightenment and the uncontrolled economic forces that now threaten us with disaster' (p. 213) is, it would seem, a race we are losing. Although these words were written in 1933, they are no less relevant today.

References

Attwood, L. (1996) 'The post-Soviet woman in the move to the market'. In R. Marsh (ed. & trans.), *Women in Russia and Ukraine* (pp. 255–66). New York: Cambridge University Press.

Becker, J. (1998) *Selling tradition: Appalachia and the construction of an American folk, 1930–1940.* Chapel Hill, NC: University of North Carolina Press.

Danchenko, L. (1982) *Folk art from the Ukraine.* A. Shkarovsky-Raffe (trans.). Leningrad: Aurora Art Publishers.

Ehler, R. D. (1995/1982) *Miners, millhands, and mountaineers: Industrialization of the Appalachian South, 1880-1930.* Knoxville, TN: University of Tennessee Press.

Ehlers, T. (1990) *Silent looms: Women and production in a Guatemalan town.* Boulder, USA: Westview Press.

Gaventa, J. (1982) *Power and powerlessness: Acquiescence and rebellion in an Appalachian Valley.* Chicago: University of Illinois Press.

Greenhalgh, P. (1997) 'The history of craft'. In P. Dormer (ed), *The culture of craft: Status and future* (pp. 20–52). New York: Manchester University Press.

Grimes, K. and Milgram, L. (2000) *Artisans and cooperatives: Developing alternative trade for the global economy.* Tucson: University of Arizona Press.

Hickey, S. and Mohan, G. (2004) 'Towards participation as transformation: critical themes and challenges'. In S. Hickey and G. Mohan (eds), *Participation: from tyranny to transformation?* (pp. 3–24). London: Zed Books.

Humphreys, R. (1999) Skilled craftswomen or cheap labour? Craft-based NGO projects as an alternative to female urban migration in northern Thailand. *Gender and Development* 7, Vol. 2, pp. 56–63.

Huseby-Darvas, E. V. (2001) Hungarian village women in the marketplace during the late socialist period. In L. Seligmann, (ed), *Women traders in cross-cultural perspective: Mediating identities, marketing wares* (pp. 185–208). Stanford, CA: Stanford University Press.

Jacobs, D. (2003) *The Myles Horton reader: Education for social change.* Knoxville, TN: University of Tennessee Press.

Kravchuk, R. S. (2002) *Ukrainian political economy: The first ten years.* New York: Palgrave Macmillan.

Littrel, M. A. and Dickson, M. A. (1999) *Social responsibility in the global market: Fair trade of cultural products.* London: Sage Publications.

Nash, J. (1992) *Crafts in the world market: The impact of global exchange on middle American artisans.* Albany, NY: State University of New York Press.

Rist, G. (2002) *The history of development: From western origins to global faith.* London: Zed books.

Salmond, W. R. (1996) *Arts and crafts in late imperial Russia: Reviving the Kustar art industries, 1870-1917.* New York: Cambridge University Press.

Seligmann, L. (2001) *Women traders in cross-cultural perspective: Mediating identities, marketing wares.* Stanford, CA: Stanford University Press.

UNESCO (2003) *Income-generating programs for poverty alleviation through non-formal education.* Bangkok, Thailand: UNESCO Asia and Pacific Regional Bureau for Education.

Whisnant, D. (1983) *All that is native & fine: The politics of culture in an American region.* Chapel Hill, NC: University of North Carolina Press.

Williams, J. A. (2002) *Appalachia: A history.* Chapel Hill, NC: University of North Carolina Press.

Index

Page numbers in bold type refer to illustrations